I'M WITH
FATTY

I'M WITH
FATTY

LOSING FIFTY POUNDS IN FIFTY MISERABLE WEEKS

EDWARD UGEL

WEINSTEIN
BOOKS

ISBN: 978-1-60286-121-3

First Edition
10   9   8   7   6   5   4   3   2

For Brooke, Sasha, & Romy

Eat or Die . . .

Contents

Introduction

There is no love sincerer than the love of food.
—George Bernard Shaw, *Man and Superman*

I'm haunted by mirrors.

Mirrors are like Kryptonite to a fat person—as are cameras. I've gained so much weight over the past few years, the last thing I want to do is see myself in a mirror or a photograph. I know how I look. I surely don't need my wife posting yet another jowly picture of me on Facebook for her 657 "friends" to enjoy. Ah, Facebook . . . how I loathe you.

Over the past four or five years, I've become a doughy, antisocial, anxiety-riddled, gray-haired monster. I've had the gray hair since college. It's the least of my concerns. Worrying about gray hair when your weight's soaring out of control is like mowing your lawn while your house is on fire. It's just silly.

I'm thirty-six years old as I write this Introduction, but I look much older. Weight does that to you. I feel old, too. Not crazy-old-man-yelling-at-birds-old—but old. I'm too young to feel this way.

Thus, the "Fatty Project" is born. Simply put, I'm attempting to lose fifty pounds over the next fifty weeks. For those of you with math skills similar to mine, that's a pound a week—2.28 ounces a day. Can I lose fifty pounds? Who knows. But I feel pretty confident about losing a few ounces a day.

The Fatty Project is a last-ditch attempt to salvage my body from the throes of obesity. As a food lover and passionate cook, I'm dreading it. As a father and husband, I know it's well past time for me to get my act together. Why now? My doctor has just informed me that I'm on a collision course with death. My wife, Brooke, is starting to panic. I can feel her fading away. She's too worried about my health to pretend that my fervent relationship with food is okay anymore. Enough is enough.

The truth of the matter is, food is more important to me than just about anything else. Project or not, I'm not sure I want that to change. Now, before folks go waving their Tony Robbins CDs at me and start ranting about the wonders of changing who you are and all that jazz—let me stop you before you lose a Birkenstock. I know I can change. I get it. I'm changing, I'm changing. Yes, anyone can change—even me. Whoop-di-do.

Right now, I simply want to lose enough weight so I don't drop dead. Everything else is of secondary importance. I'm not starting this project to look good with my shirt off. I stopped believing I could feel comfortable at the beach a long time ago—never have, never will. When it comes down to it, for me food trumps having a great body—or even a pretty good one.

But as much as I love food, I love my wife and two daughters more . . . I think. I want to be healthy so I can watch my girls grow up. I want to grow old with my wife. I want to be there for all of them as long as possible.

That said, I have no intention of growing old by eating nothing but whole grains and steamed broccoli. I simply refuse. Food makes me happy. We're a package deal. I live to eat. I love to eat at restaurants. I love to cook. I love the social component of eating. To me, food is culture—at least it's my culture. I can't be happy without being a social eater. And, if I could, I wouldn't want to be. I need food in my social life, more than I ever thought.

I grew up thinking that getting healthy or going on a diet was an all-or-nothing proposition. My family's diets were always urgent. Diet or else. I never grew up hearing anyone say that they were going on a manageable, realistic diet. I carried that mind-set with me into adulthood. Thus, I've spent much of the last decade breaking epic diets. Each new diet was going to be the one that changed everything, the one to make up for the previous six during which I was weak and undisciplined. Every diet I've ever started had so much pressure on it to be a smash hit, it was doomed to fail.

Every time I've started a diet, it's been with the same thought in mind—lose every ounce of fat on my body—look like I did back in high school—shock my friends and family with my stick-to-itiveness—hit the beach without wanting to wear a burka—get into my skinny jeans. Yes, men have skinny jeans.

This all-or-nothing mind-set has had a ruinous effect on me—both as an eater and a dieter. I can't just have one or two scoops of ice cream. Not me. I eat the entire pint. A little hasn't been good enough for quite some time. Just one slice of pizza? Yeah, right. Forgo the appetizer tonight? What are you, a Commie? It's as if I'm having an affair, but my mistress isn't that redhead from *Mad Men,* it's two bowls of ice cream and a wedge of cold pizza. I haven't always been like this—so obsessed with eating. Why now? What happened?

My goal this year is to figure that out. I want to re-learn how to eat. I want to continue to cook and eat interesting food, but in normal, or even small, portions. There are worse things than small portions of delicious food—like huge portions of steamed asparagus and skin-less poached chicken breast. I think I can live by these rules—literally and figuratively.

For years, I've been rewarding myself with food. But until now, I never really asked myself what I was rewarding myself for. If I've been healthy for a few days, or a few weeks, I can feel the pressure mounting in my mind . . . it's time for a reward. If I've been good, Tubby needs a treat. Conversely, if I've had a bad day, if I've already gone off my latest diet, why not give in to the little voice in my head convincing me that it's already too late? Go ahead . . . have a little something . . . have a lot of something . . *eat, Bubbe, eat.*

Before I dive too deep into my story, I should let you

know a little bit about me. I grew up the middle of five children in Rockville, Maryland, just outside of Washington, DC, in a typical suburban neighborhood called Flower Valley. My father is a doctor and my mother was a teacher but stayed at home with us until we were in high school. Our backyard had a pool, a garden, and a giant weeping willow tree whose wispy branches would scrape against the window in the bedroom I shared with my brother Phil, scaring us silly throughout our childhood. To this day, every time I see a weeping willow, I feel the urge to crawl into bed with my brother or wet my pants.

I was a "lifer" at a local Quaker school, Sidwell Friends School, meaning that I attended from kindergarten all the way through the twelfth grade. It was there that I fell in love with books, art, drama, and storytelling. I also learned how to sit in a silent Quaker meeting for forty-five minutes without passing gas. Other than turning me into a foaming-at-the-mouth pacifist, the biggest impact the school had on me was introducing me to my wife.

Brooke and I have known each other for most of our lives. She is two years younger than me. I was an old, salty-dog first grader by the time she arrived in kindergarten. We dated a bit in high school, but we weren't exactly high school sweethearts. To the contrary, we both dated other people for most of high school and college. Yet, somehow, we always came back to each other.

Brooke can see the beauty in everyone. She has such a big heart that it just slays me. I barely like anyone. And, while I play the role of distracted, antisocial grizzly bear to rave reviews, she's taught me how to live in the present and enjoy the blessings I have. (I'm a work in progress.) She's a psychotherapist now in private practice here in Bethesda, Maryland. She spent years working in public clinics with folks who otherwise couldn't afford therapy. During all those years when I was out there trying to make a buck, she was in the community trying to make people's lives better.

I spent the good part of a decade bluffing my way up the corporate ladder and quickly found myself near the top of a finance company's hierarchy and payroll. While it was a role I had never expected to play, I became a successful salesman and manager. Early in 2006, I was fired. (More on that later.) I was thirty-three years old. Rather than move into another business and continue on the corporate path, I jumped off a cliff and became a freelance writer and author. (What is the sound of one wife gasping?)

In case you're wondering how you become a freelance writer, it's actually quite simple:

1. Quit or get fired from your job.
2. Inform your wife of brilliant plan to write for a living, despite the fact that you've never once been paid to write so much as an e-mail.
3. Sit through an incredibly awkward dinner with your in-laws informing them of same.
4. Spend the next three or four years "being witty" in your basement.

5. Slowly bleed out your savings.
6. Refuse to call yourself a stay-at-home dad because, unlike *those* guys, *you* stay at home to work, not hang out with your kids.
7. Stay at home and hang out with your kids.
8. *Voilà!* You're a freelance writer.

Back in the day, I made quite a nice living in the business world. Consequently, Brooke and I did what every rising finance guy and his spouse do—we bought a big house in the suburbs. The mortgage wasn't a problem, not for a big shot like me. But for a neophyte writer, it's . . . not such a great fit. So here we are in a beautiful house we can no longer afford, with a former corporate senior vice president now writing for a "living." Do I like it here in Bethesda? When I'm not consumed with the stress of trying to pay the bills, yes. It's very nice. The noose around my neck is made of velvet. Lucky me.

Money issues notwithstanding, these days I live a peaceful, happy life. I'm happily married and I have two healthy daughters who make me laugh and beam with pride every day. And, unlike 99 percent of the men I know, I've actually been around to see these two girls grow. Sasha was nine months old when I left corporate life. She'll be five in May. Romy is two. I'm here when they wake up. I'm here when they go to bed. I'm here. I'm here for them and they're here for me. I'd eat glass for one of my old paychecks, and I miss the health benefits and the security of a more traditional job, but nothing compares to being with these two girls every day. No matter how much money you have, you only get one shot at being a dad. I can honestly say that I've made the most of it. I wouldn't change a thing. Oh, except the part about being fat.

Chapter 1

I'm at the age where food has taken the place of sex in my life. In fact, I just had a mirror put over my kitchen table.

—*Rodney Dangerfield*

August is an insufferable time of year in Bethesda, Maryland. Once the cherry blossoms have come and gone, a dense blanket of heat and humidity falls on the city and doesn't let up until well past Labor Day. During the late summer, there is little to enjoy in town besides local blue crabs and good central air-conditioning. Other than that, you'd be just as happy baking in the sun down in Florida. At least there, everybody's got a pool.

During the height of the summer, I usually try to stay indoors as much as possible. For a six-foot-two guy who just recently surged past 260 pounds, the heat makes sweat pour out of me like Albert Brooks in *Broadcast News*. But with two young daughters, like it or not, I'm outside all the time.

We have one of those $14.99 Toys "R" Us plastic pools in our backyard. Unfortunately, Sasha and Romy cry every time I try to get in with them. It drives me crazy.

One day last August, I made a big show out of throwing the back door open, stripping down to my boxers, and jumping into the pool. Thinking I'd get some credit for my wacky-dad-jumps-in-pool routine, I was met instead with the shrieks of two terrified girls and a familiar look of disgust from my wife, Brooke. The fact that half the pool's water had spilled out onto the deck didn't help my cause.

"This is OUR pool, Daddy!" Sasha yelled.

"Edward, get out of the goddamn pool." Brooke added. "They're upset."

"There's no more water," Sasha added. "You're too big. Mommy—he's *too* big!"

I was too big.

With my feelings hurt, and my ego bruised, I got out of the pool and threw some early childhood guilt at Sasha.

"Daddy *bought* the pool. You're not sharing with me. That makes me feel bad. How about I take it back to the store, or give the pool to a girl who wants to share with her daddy?" I said, trying to maintain the illusion of being a grown-up.

"Very helpful, honey," Brooke said. "Thanks for stopping by."

"She was mean to me first!"

"She's four."

"There's still such a thing as manners."

"Edward, go inside."

I could not wait for the cool fronts of autumn.

My kid was correct. My eating had gotten entirely out of hand. I spent the entire month of August frantically eating like a bear prepping for hibernation. In fact, August was a full-blown disaster. What exactly happened? I gained ten pounds. *(He bows and waves to the crowd.)*

I'm told gaining ten pounds in such a short period of time is actually quite hard to pull off. Normally, someone who gains that much weight in a month is either pregnant, trying to win a bar bet, or preparing for their role in *Raging Bull*. For the rest of us—it's not viewed as an accomplishment.

That night in bed, Brooke finally brought it up. She not only pointed out that there was an elephant in the room, she took aim and shot at it.

"We've got to talk about what's happening with your weight."

"Is this because of what happened in the pool today?"

"Are you serious?"

"Sasha was rude to *me*."

"A child, your child, was rude to you?"

"Yes . . . she made me feel fat."

"Honey . . ."

"What? I *am* fat? Is that the point?"

"I'm not calling you fat. But I am concerned about you."

"I'm just, I don't know . . . in a bit of a funk."

"A funk?"

"No good? You're not buying the whole 'funk' thing? I thought it had a shot—"

"—I want you to hear something."

Brooke reached into her nightstand and pulled out my microcassette recorder—never a good thing. I quickly went through a horrifying montage of all the things that could be on the recorder. It was a coin toss whether or not to simply listen or smash the recorder to pieces and jump out the window like Chief in *One Flew Over the Cuckoo's Nest*. Thinking better of it, I did as she requested and pressed play.

The recording sounded like an animal doing something unseemly—perhaps having sex, killing and eating its prey, or slowly dying. Whatever it was, I felt sorry for it and quietly hoped it was done suffering.

"What *is* that?"

"It's you."

"Me? What am I doing, protecting my cubs from hunters?"

"You're snoring."

"Impossible."

"That's why I recorded it. It's unbelievable."

"How long does it go on?"

"Forever."

"What do you make of it?"

"I think it's because of all the . . . I think it's weight-related."

"I never snored before?"

"Not like this. This is something entirely different. This seems . . . medical."

"Medical?"

"I googled it."

"You googled 'snoring'?"

"I googled 'snoring and weight gain.'"

"What'd it say?"

"It says we need to talk to a doctor."

It's not that Brooke was tired of walking around with a fluffier version of me. It wasn't my jowls or the closet-ful of clothes that no longer fit me. It was the snoring. In the end, the snoring did me in. You can't maintain the il-lusion that everything's under control when you're fast asleep.

As was often the case during the months since our second daughter was born, I blamed Brooke for my less-than-per-fect mood. No doubt, she blamed me for hers, too. In the dog days of our sixth year of marriage, we spent our time juggling poopy diapers and burp cloths, and muttering sarcastic comments under our breath. At night, when our two beautiful daughters were asleep, we'd do our best not to suffocate each other with a pillow. Luckily, with a three-month-old baby, you always sleep with one eye open. Every time I even thought about smothering Brooke, she knowingly told me to stop fidgeting and go to sleep.

Yes, dear.

We were no longer newlyweds. We were simply mar-ried people. This was a cold war. She was winning. Dé-tente would likely come only once the new baby was off to college. Until then, we were North and South Korea.

Despite the recent . . . tensions, Brooke was still my best friend. I can't help it—I like my wife. She's the one I first want to speak with when things go right, and the per-son I lean on when things go wrong. Either way, I want her by my side. Fiercely loyal and eerily well-organized, she's the ideal counterbalance to my chaotic self. She's the Lucy to my Pig-Pen—if Lucy weren't such a raving bitch.

As either of my two chins would tell you, I'm cursed with bad genes. Every time I eat a sandwich, it sticks to me like glue. Brooke, on the other hand, is graced with a beautiful, curvy body tied together with a tight, flat tummy. Even after two kids, she's got the same body she had in high school. She's actually more beautiful today than she was when we first started dating. She's aging like Meryl Streep. I, however, look more like Henry Kissinger with every passing hour. She got the short end of the stick in this marriage. I'm walking around like a lottery winner with her on my arm. She's stuck with a socially awkward Mr. Snuffleupagus for the rest of her life. On the bright side, I'm a good cook and I've made the playoffs in my fantasy football league two out of the past fourteen years. So, I'm quite a catch myself.

Brooke's a natural beauty, with flawless skin and big brown eyes—think the best parts of Tina Fey and Jennifer Grey. She's also so damn nice to everyone, it drives me absolutely batty. I spend a substantial part of my life trying not to despise everyone who walks on two feet. Brooke sees the good in everyone—even me. How can she love this doughy, annoyed malcontent? Her goodness, set against my badness, well, it absolutely mystifies me. Yet in those long, hot days of August, I found myself pushing her further and further away. It's hard to love someone when you barely like yourself—even if that someone is your doting wife.

What a mess I make of things.

Brooke was genuinely concerned about me. In fact, she was scared. And she had a right to be. After she consulted our family doctor, she learned that I was probably not just snoring too much, but suffering from sleep apnea. Sleep apnea is when you stop breathing while you sleep. The kicker? If you do it long enough—stop breathing—you die from heart failure. Not good. Brooke had decided to light a match to shed some light on my sleeping issues and was handed back a stick of dynamite instead. Serves her right.

Boom.

I never used to snore. It only started a few years ago, when I began gaining weight as if I were raising money by the pound for charity. Like everyone else, I have always hated snoring. I consider it a major character flaw, like chewing with your mouth open. Once, I even refused to share a room with one of my best friends on our annual Vegas trip because his snoring ruined the precious few hours of sleep you get out there. Suddenly it was looking like I'd be the sad sack with my own room in Vegas. Brooke *had* to put up with my snoring. My best friends spending the weekend with me? Not a chance. Fifty-fifty odds say they'd wheel the sleeping me onto the elevator and send me down to the casino level to get arrested in my underwear. I, no doubt, would do the very same to them.

Of course, our family doctor just happens to be good-looking and charming and generally a great guy. Dr. Williams is in his early forties, has a few kids of his own, and is the spitting image of Joel McHale, who hosts *The Soup* on E! Odds are that the good doctor doesn't snore at all, much less snore *and* stop breathing—scaring the hell out of his wife every night. I wish *I* were married to him, so I wouldn't be surprised if the thought has crossed Brooke's mind a time or two. I'm sure it just killed her to confide in Dr. Wonderful about me.

Once he realized that I might have sleep apnea, Brooke said Dr. Williams acted all worried about me, completely freaking her out—laying the foundation for her to move on to an eventual life without me. I, the elephant not in the room, wasn't there to hear what was said or defend myself. That was probably for the best, because I'd likely have gotten all pouty and defensive, making Dr. Williams' case against me that much stronger. It was an intervention without the patient—just two caring, non-snoring, thin, happy people with postgraduate degrees standing there in the examination room—all full of concern and straight teeth and great eyes and diplomas on the wall. Get a room.

Dr. Williams said that my way out of the snoring mess started with a mandatory field trip to the Center for Sleep and Wake Disorders in Chevy Chase, Maryland. This would include a night sleeping under the watchful eye of a lab technician, a myriad of computers, and several beeping machines. Together, they would break down my sleep habits and report the data back to Dr. Williams. What specifically would they look for? They wanted to know if I stopped breathing while I slept. If so, how often? Did they care about the snoring? Sure, but more out of empathy for my wife. In reality, snoring isn't going to kill anyone except if, out of frustration, your wife whacks you over the head with a frying pan. The sleep apnea actually can.

When I finally went to see Dr. Williams myself, he assured me that I needed to do the overnight test. He promised me that he wasn't just taking Brooke's side. He promised me that if I didn't, I was at risk of not making it past forty. He added that, on a personal note, from the way my wife was talking, it was either the sleep center or the guest room in my basement. Dr. Williams had a point. I needed to do this both for myself and for the good of my marriage.

Clearly, I was going to the sleep study. Apparently, I was going soon. Unbeknownst to me, Brooke had already made an appointment for that Sunday night—the same night the Bears were playing the Colts in Indianapolis. So much for football.

Standing in the sleep center's elevator on Sunday night, I could feel the blood falling out of my face. This was getting serious. I was alone, and I'm not my best audience. Normally at a time like this, when I'm scared, I'll make jokes to Brooke or anyone else who will listen. I'd joke my way through this—as I do most everything else. Anything to keep me from thinking about what's waiting upstairs. I knew I'd walk out the next morning with paperwork documenting what I'd known for some time—I was fat and I was in trouble. Right now there was no punch line, no water-squirting flower, no spit take. Once those elevator doors opened on the seventeenth floor, Fatty's not so funny.

The Center for Sleep and Wake Disorders claims to be "a full service sleep center caring for patients with all disorders of sleep and wakefulness." Translation: if it keeps you up or makes you tired, they deal with it . . . as long as you've got the cash.

On the seventeenth floor, a technician opened the door to the sleep center and asked my name without saying so much as hello. I was the latest in a long line of fat guys to come for this slumber party. Still, what gives? I know it wasn't the Four Seasons, but the sleep center was charging me $700 for this goddamn room—$700 my insurance company told me they wouldn't be covering. So I think a smile and a "welcome to the worst night of your life," or at least a "hiya" wouldn't have been asking too much.

I was shown to a reception desk. There were four other technicians milling about doing various tasks. They were all dressed in matching khakis and blue golf shirts with the company's logo on the breast. They looked like the graveyard shift at Best Buy. Check-in was virtually the same as at any hotel. Yet the air tubes, face masks, and electronic gadgets lying about didn't exactly give off a Marriott vibe. I was in my very own canto of hell.

I peeked down the hall and saw two heavyset older men fecklessly looking for their rooms—think James Gandolfini and John Madden. They'd obviously been there for a while, because they were both wearing pajamas and already had wires and electrodes attached to their bodies.

They were just walking the halls dragging all these cords behind them. To complete the ensemble, they were both wearing dress socks and slippers. It's not a good look. In fact, it was frighteningly surreal. These were my roommates. It hit me like a sucker punch . . . *These are my roommates?* Holy Christ! What have I done to myself? All the other guys who were being forced by their wives, children, or doctors to sleep in a cage were my dad's age—or older. There was no one in there vaguely within spitting distance of my age. I wasn't expecting to have to see anyone else when I got there, much less men who looked so old, so out of shape . . . so much like me. I wanted out, but there was no way Brooke would let me in the house if I left. I was there to make her happy. If I left, she'd be plenty upset and a bit panicked, too. Like it or not, I was staying.

They put me in Room 10, the one closest to the reception area. It had a twin bed, some hooks to hang up my clothes, and a sink surrounded by all kinds of tubes and ointments. That's it. Basically, it looked like a massage parlor . . . or so I'm told. There was no TV, no phone, no toilet, no Brooke, nothing.

The guy checking me in mentioned in passing that this was the worst room because it was unbearably hot. Admittedly, it's an interesting sales technique, simply stating that the room sucks. And all this for $700. He quickly added that they were all booked up so they couldn't move me to another room. Perfect.

He wasn't kidding. It was hot in there. The air was stale, pungent. It smelled like they'd been cooking curry just behind the wall to my room. Perhaps the smell was left over from last night's fat guy. Maybe he ordered take-out. Could we do that here? I was curious but way too intimidated to ask.

I would have complained to the management about the heat and the smell and the lack of a happy-hour buffet if I hadn't been so totally mortified to be there in the first place. Making a stink right now, since I was about to be in their hands for the rest of the night while they glued electrodes all over my body, didn't seem the wise play.

I was told to sit down and wait for my technician to come back. "Feel free to make yourself comfortable," he said. I considered pooping on the floor.

Instead, I waited in the curried heat and stared at the door. I wondered what the tech would look like. Was it someone I'd seen out front? Was it a man or a woman? I prayed that it was a man—a big, boring man.

Not quite.

My tech walked into the room. She was gorgeous. She was a sexy giggle machine not a day over twenty-four. Her name was Margaux, pronounced as if you were a French bartender, not Forrest Gump. She had beautiful caramel skin and emerald green eyes. Plus, she laughed at everything I said. She couldn't seem to help herself. I was apparently adorable. It became clear that my night, which was supposed to be spent trying to save my life, would undoubtedly be derailed by me making jokes and trying to impress her. Perhaps she'd like to split a pizza?

Talking to a beautiful woman, much less actually saying something charming, has always been tough for me. I'm insanely insecure, and this scene, the sleep clinic, where I was the fat patient, wasn't exactly teeing me up. What was she going to find most seductive, the wedding ring wedged onto my fat finger? My size 40 pants, which were conspicuously unbuttoned—my belt the only thing keeping them from falling to the floor? Any one of my chins? My man boobs? Exactly which of these qualities should I try to highlight in the brief time we had before she tucked me into bed like a sickly child?

"I have to measure your nostrils," she said.

"My what? Why?"

I flashed back in a photo montage of the 8,941 times I'd picked my nose prior to that moment. I think I picked my nose in the car on the way over—and again on the elevator. Damn boogers. I wish I could quit you.

She came at my nose with some sort of sadistic measuring device to gauge exactly what she was up against.

"My nose has an apology letter from my grandfather in my bag."

"Tell your nose it's charming . . ."

"It thinks you're just saying that to be nice."

"It's very distinguished."

"Like Jimmy Durante . . ."

"I don't know who that is."

"He's a point guard for the Knicks."

"Oh, cool."

So she wasn't the girl of my dreams. That was likely for the best.

"You're gonna need a large-sized nose piece."

"What? You sure I'm not a medium?" My voice quivered . . . *I'm so cool.*

"I wish," she said, completely serious. "Ain't happening."

Our date was going well. She was going to love my parents.

Before Margaux started attaching all manner of wires and electrodes to my body, she explained that I had to choose between one of two different styles of CPAP mask. A CPAP is a machine that shoots a constant stream of air directly into your nose. It stops the soft palate (the flappy thing in the back of your throat that makes you snore) from wiggling around. When you snore, the soft palate flops around like an unhinged screen door in a windstorm. When you're wearing the CPAP mask, the second the flap falls down, the air from the machine knocks it right back into place. It's not as technically savvy as an iPhone, but it certainly works. No flapping, no snoring.

When you wear the CPAP mask, you're supposed to inhale and exhale through your nose, something I find extremely hard to do. Why can't you breathe through your mouth? Because when you do, the air being pumped up your nose makes an awkward U-turn and comes screaming uncontrollably out of your mouth, accompanied by a vicious hissing sound. It's exactly like the sound the suction hook at the dentist's makes when it's getting all the saliva out of your mouth. *Make love to me, Margaux. . . .*

The CPAP machine itself sat on a table and was attached to an air tube, which connected to the face mask that was now strapped to my head. She was outfitting this absurd elephant's tusk to properly hang off my face, but I was still hamming it up for her. I looked like that fat guy who flies Starfighters with Luke Skywalker at the end of *Star Wars*. He's the one who dies just before Luke shoots his blaster into the Death Star. The fat guy dies. How original.

Of the two mask styles from which I could choose, the first looked exactly like a men's athletic cup sitting upside down over my nose. I passed. The second had two stubby air tubes which fit snugly *inside* my nostrils. The benefit? There's no actual cup covering the majority of your face. The negatives? Imagine having Joe Garagiola's thumbs jammed up your nose. It was so uncomfortable, so alien, that I suddenly understood the draw of option one.

Pressured to make a decision, I chose the mask with the nostril tubes—the lesser of two absolute evils. Margaux fit it on my head using Velcro and a chin strap. Yes, from now on, I was to wear a chin strap to bed. It was a nightmare. I sneaked a glance at myself in the mirror. I wondered what my kids would think if they could see me. Would they laugh or cry? And what about Brooke? This little contraption would do nothing to spice up our love life. What the hell was she supposed to think should I have to strap this baby on at night? *Paging Barry White.*

I told Margaux that I looked ridiculous. She quickly agreed with me. She added that I should wear the mask to the grocery store so I could park in a handicap space. Charming.

This was the plan for the rest of the night: I was

supposed to fall asleep with all these wires and electrodes taped and glued to my scalp, chest, belly, and knees. If I actually fell asleep, they would monitor my sleep habits without the CPAP mask for a few hours. If I didn't show signs of sleep apnea, they'd let me sleep through the night and that would be that. If I showed signs of sleep apnea, Margaux would come in and make me put on the mask. In essence, if they wake you up, you're in trouble.

As she made final preparations before turning off the lights, I informed her that I was going to be one of the lucky ones, the data buster, the sleep-through-the-night guy. As she slid the door shut, she whispered back, "Good luck with that." I was starting to hate her.

The room was now pitch-black, but I knew they were watching me. Not only were they watching—they were taking notes. They were judging me and laughing and drinking sodas and having an all-around good time at my expense. Tomorrow, they'd share the results with my doctor, who would make me wear this sadistic clown mask to bed for the rest of my life.

Lying there in the dark, knowing the staff was right outside, knowing they could measure my heartbeat, my oxygen levels, et cetera, I'd never been so self-conscious in my life. For Maryland's most self-conscious man, that was really saying something. The night-vision camera's red eye stared down at me from the ceiling. I stared back in depressed horror and tried to imagine a less appropriate time to masturbate than right there, right then. Finally, I drifted off to sleep.

After what seemed like only a few minutes, Margaux

came in and told me that I had to put on the mask. She said I was "well over the limit of acceptable results." I scurried to write down her words, because I knew I wouldn't remember them in a few hours.

"How long was I asleep?"

"About two hours."

"How bad was it?"

"Bad."

"Bad enough to need a machine at home?"

"Bad enough for your wife to move out."

"Do you know something I don't?"

"No. Just a hunch."

With that middle-of-the-night-insult placed squarely in my lap, she shoved the tubes into my nostrils, tightened my Velcro chin strap, told me to breathe through my nose, and walked out of the room.

And there I was, in that dark room, all by myself.

There were two plastic tubes shoved deep inside my nose, blowing cool air into my brain so I didn't drop dead. I was thirty-six years old. What had I done to myself? For the first time in my life, I was scared of being fat. This wasn't about looking good or fitting into an old suit. This wasn't about having the confidence to walk into a bar without feeling like everyone was measuring my love handles. This wasn't funny. This was life support. This was literally life support. I *was* the elephant in the room.

I didn't end up there because of my genes. I didn't end up there because I fell ill. This wasn't some bad hand of cards that I'd been dealt. I was there because I wouldn't stop eating. I did it to myself. It didn't have to happen.

With the slightest bit of control, I wouldn't have been there. I wanted to cry. If I hadn't been completely convinced that one single tear would electrocute every single inch of me, that's just what I would have done. For the second time, I fell asleep trying to imagine lying next to my wife with this monstrosity hanging off my face. I never wanted to eat again.

At dawn, Margaux woke me up with all the tenderness of a drill sergeant and told me I could leave. Reality had set in, and I was done playing the silly fool. I was too spent. Plus, like any good psychotic, I'd decided to place the blame for my situation squarely at her feet. I hated her now. This was all her fault. I imagine that, after listening to me snore the night away, she was just about done with me, too. We barely spoke as she pulled all the wires off my body. It was awkward. I wanted out. Worst one-night stand . . . ever.

Before I left, she asked me to fill out a survey. I checked off the boxes in random order and didn't go out of my way to write anything nice. I grabbed my stuff and headed toward the door. As I made my way out, I heard her mumble, "Enjoy your CPAP machine," under her breath.

Traitor.

Two weeks later, I was looking for my grandfather's old leatherwork hole punch. Once again, I'd outgrown my fat belt, my "in case of emergency" belt. My closet offered no further solutions. This belt *was* the solution. At this point, it was the leather punch or the Big and Tall store near the mall. There's nothing I like less than going to the Big and Tall store. To date, I'd been only once—okay, three times. Shameful, that place. Everyone there is sad, embarrassed, or both—it's a little like the waiting room at my shrink's office. The Big and Tall store is where you go when you've broken every promise to yourself, when all else has failed, when the only comfortable wardrobe offerings in your closet come with drawstrings or elastic. It's where you go when there's nowhere else to go.

I had a follow-up appointment with Dr. Williams that day and I was desperate for a pair of pants that actually fit, in case he asked me to take off my shirt. The last thing I needed at that point was for my own doctor to see firsthand that I could no longer button my size 40 pants. It wouldn't go over well when I was still trying to convince him that I didn't need to sleep with the medical equivalent of a dunce cap strapped to my face. If nothing else, I should show up in a pair of pants that fit.

Dr. Williams had already reviewed the data from the sleep center. I knew what the numbers were going to say. I knew what this appointment was really about. I was about to get a big pep talk about how great the CPAP machine is, how it was going to change my life and all that crap. The bottom line was, he was going to make me promise to wear it, and I was going to say yes. I had to say yes if I wanted to stay married and, perhaps, live past football season.

As always, Dr. Williams was great. He blew into the room like a magician at a kid's birthday party—all full of life and energy. I admit—it was infectious. He was all pumped up, so I got pumped up. He told me all kinds of bad news from the sleep study, but his Zig Ziglar delivery worked beautifully. I was apparently dying, but I was enjoying the hell out of our conversation. Dr. Williams told me that if I didn't do something about this body soon, I'd die. He actually used those words to describe my situation: *Ed, fat, crisis, death.* Being called fat wasn't the least bit surprising to me. I own a mirror. But when he said the words *crisis* and *death*, all the air left the room. I was caught off guard. I felt about a hundred years old. I felt scared. I wanted a meatball sandwich.

The data said that while I sleep, I stop breathing to the point of turning blue once every minute.

Once every minute I'm turning blue.

I was literally suffocating myself under the weight of all that fat. He said the CPAP machine would add years to my life. He said I was playing Russian roulette if I didn't wear it. He said I had to wear it or he'd stop being my doctor. For all his threats, there was just one thing that I couldn't get out of my head: the look on my wife's face when she saw me wearing this thing for the first time. I can find another doctor, but there's only one Brooke.

I did the math. It wasn't pretty. There were precious few angles here, no real corners to cut, not a lot of wiggle room to sell my side of the story. Still, I thought I might have a way out of this mess. It wasn't a quick fix, and it couldn't be bought. I'd have to earn it. I hated the idea of earning it. What if I got healthy? Could I make all this go away if I got in shape? Was that even an option?

Scared to know the answer, I asked Dr. Williams the big question.

"If I lose weight, will I still have to wear the mask?"

"I'm not sure, but there's a real chance you won't."

"A real chance? Or are you bullshitting me so I'll wear it?"

"A little of both."

"How little?"

"If you lose a significant amount of weight, your snoring will definitely get better, no question."

"Quantify *significant*."

"How much have you gained this year?"

"Let's say fifty pounds."

"Jesus, Ed! Do you have any idea how bad that is for your body?"

"The thought has crossed my mind, yes."

"Lose those fifty pounds and you'll lose the mask."

"Do you promise?"

"Absolutely not."

"I'll take that as a yes."

"Don't."

"Too late. You promised."

For the 32,139th time, I was lying to myself. Nothing new there. However, this time, for the first time, it was for my own good. I was pretending that my doctor made me a promise that he never really made. After all, what else did I have right then if not hope—even false hope? To borrow a phrase, I guess I was the change I'd been waiting for. Who knew.

I couldn't fathom a future where this mask was a permanent fixture in my life. I'd go mad. I had to hold on to the notion, even if it was largely made up, that losing all that weight would not only save my life, but more importantly, it would mean throwing out that goddamn CPAP mask. And, in the end, if I was wrong, if I lost the weight and I still had sleep apnea . . . well, so what. What are you going to do? Worse comes to worse, it was better to wear a gas mask to bed weighing 213 pounds than 263. At 263 pounds, the CPAP mask was the straw that broke the camel's back. It was simply asking too much of my wife. Completely fat *and* the mask? No. She shouldn't have to suffer through that, not even for me. But, a lean, muscular 213 pounds along with the mask? Well, that was a whole different story. I'd be like Tom Cruise in *Top Gun* with that thing on my face. At the very least, I'd look like Goose, and I can settle for that. Goose never accused Matt Lauer of being glib.

And so began my journey to get that mask off my face. First, however, before I got rid of the mask, I had to worry about the one I'd already been wearing around for all these years. There are all kinds of masks—different ways to hide behind a character. For as long as I can remember, I've played the role of the funny fat guy—brilliantly, mind you. I have always believed—or hoped—that if you make folks laugh, they won't notice your girth. I've spent a lifetime joking away the pain that comes with this body. Well, looking in the mirror, it seemed the joke was on me.

I wasn't looking for a life-changing transformation. I didn't want to go on *Oprah* in a bikini. I didn't want to impress everyone at my twentieth high school reunion the following year. I probably wouldn't be going anyway. I just wanted the American dream: to sleep like a normal guy again so my wife could see my face when she refused to have sex with me.

Chapter 2

I haven't a particle of confidence in a man who has no redeeming petty vices.

—*Mark Twain*

Starting a real diet after so many years of eating anything I wanted was akin to turning around a cruise ship. It took a while to get it going in the right direction. I had only a minimal plan for the first day:

> Step one—Put down the Twinkies.
> Step two—Shave my beautiful double-chin-hiding
> depression beard.
> Step three—Panic.

Why shave the beard? Like Al Gore after the 2000 election, I grew it in a somewhat transparent attempt to hide from the outside world. Shaving it off was a way to start over. This project is about examining and ultimately erasing the lies I tell myself every day. It's all this covering up that's killing me. Pretending that I'm okay has done me nothing but harm. I'm not okay. So, if I'm really going to look at myself, the beard had to go. Plus, my wife said so.

Brooke took the dreaded "before" photo of me with my beard. She practically dragged me by the ear to stand outside on our deck so she could take my picture. I think all these months of watching me fall apart, watching me gain so much weight while she sat there biting her tongue finally got to her. If I wasn't going to start this diet on the right foot, she was going to start it for me.

The photo shoot, the location, the shave, the date—it was all her idea. If I had my druthers, I'd have watched the Nationals game. I was getting around to the diet and the exercise. What was her big rush? I tried to smile in the photo, but you can see the sadness in my eyes. Apparently, the diet was starting today. I wasn't ready. Brooke was. She took her pictures and promptly sent me upstairs to shave my beard. I felt like Linus when he lost his woobie. Yes, ma'am.

If you've never grown a beard you're either:

a) Happy
b) Gainfully employed
c) A woman
d) Thin

The depression beard was a vacation from reality. The beard symbolized many things: complete surrender, a declaration of independence, an absolute loss of interest in a social life, and a Thoreau-like (or perhaps Unabomber) need to be left alone for a while. The heavier I got, the less I wanted to remember who I was, what I looked like, or what I used to look like not too long ago. If I could have grown fur around my entire body, I would have. The beard was as close as I could get.

My oldest kid, Sasha, was never a fan of the beard. She asked me to shave it nearly every day. I'll typically do anything for my kids, yet stubbornly, I kept the beard. Like Steve Martin schlepping that chair and ashtray around in *The Jerk,* the beard was all I had.

My beard was a mask, a costume, makeup. I'd been wearing mine for the last nine months while I pretended that my life was under control. In fact, my life had become a total train wreck. I'd let things go. My wife lost faith in me, and sadly, so had I. The beard, well, it took the edge off. At least I could be *that guy,* "wacky bearded guy." It wasn't much to hold on to in the middle of this self-inflicted storm I was weathering and dragging my family through—but it was all I had. I was surrounded by a loving family, but I felt totally alone. I'd been whistling past the graveyard when it came to my ever-increasing health problems for nearly a year. Everyone seemed to think I'd simply given up. Even our cat kept her distance. Then, she died—no kidding.

In the bathroom, I stared at the scissors, shaving cream, and lonely razor for a few minutes, trying to find the courage to lather up and get going. Finally, an epiphany: What about a nice, trimmed goatee? At least a goatee would cover up some of my face while still satisfying my promise of a fresh start. Delighted with my plan, I spent the next half hour transforming from well-fed Neanderthal to hipster goateed sex symbol. Thinking I'd pulled off a coup of sorts, I practically floated downstairs to show Brooke my new face. She was not pleased.

"Um, no. No way."

"What? No good?"

"No good. It's not what you promised, and . . . it's not you."

"What do you mean it's not me? It's me. Ta-da! I can pull this off."

"I hate it."

"Hate?"

"Hate."

Annoyed, I went back upstairs and decided to teach her a lesson. If she didn't like my goatee, let's see how she liked a moustache. I proceeded to shave the goatee into the most wonderful 1970s moustache imaginable. I came back downstairs looking like a porn version of The Cheshire Cat. Unfortunately, Brooke called my bluff and told me she loved it. Knowing that we were having friends over for dinner in a few hours, the game of chicken had officially begun.

I looked like Tom Selleck's idiot cousin. I desperately wanted to shave. But, as insecure as I am, I'm doubly stubborn. I wasn't going to shave the moustache until she begged me to do so. Counting on my social anxiety to start kicking in, Brooke wasn't budging.

Down in the kitchen, I started to prep some rainbow trout that I was going to grill for dinner—not a word from Brooke. I began to trim some artichokes, getting them ready to steam before finishing them on the grill. Nothing.

I was down to halving and pitting some peaches—also for the grill, the last bit of prep work before our friends arrived. Time was running out. Brooke was entrenched. As a last resort, I cornered her and planted a big kiss on her lips. Unfazed, she kissed me back—harder than usual.

"Yummy. It's like having a quickie with Burt Reynolds."

"I'm your male fantasy come to life."

"Yes. I can finally cross 'kissing an idiot' off my to-do list."

"I like it."

"So, keep it."

"I hate it . . ."

"Me too."

"Think I can shave it off before everyone gets here?"

"God, I hope so."

Even now that I've started the Fatty Project, there is surprisingly little relief. The stress over my weight, the ensuing health problems, the CPAP mask, and what the possibility of my dying meant to my family, trumped the excitement about starting the diet. There was no launch party, no announcement, no breaking a bottle of champagne across the bow of a ship. Doing so would have felt like spiking the ball when your team's down by thirty points.

Stupidly, I decided to start the actual diet while vacationing in a small, crowded cabin in Maine with my in-laws. I ended up having to discuss my plans for getting healthy with Brooke's family even though, at that point, I had absolutely no idea what I was talking about. The lack of privacy in that cabin reminded me of the bathrooms at summer camp when I was a kid. The bathrooms were simply gutted cabins with two rows of toilets, maybe a foot apart, not a door or wall in sight. There was no divider, no privacy, no dignity in that place. You could literally hold hands with the poor bastard sitting next to you while you took a crap, which I must say is not a good idea—even if you were totally kidding. No one ever found that nearly as funny as I did.

For months leading up to that trip to Maine, everyone kept asking me when the actual diet portion of the project was going to start. I'd often have to resist responding to the offending party by kicking them in the groin. Being asked about my weight, or when I might be starting a new diet, is emotionally crippling; the person might as well show me a picture of myself in the white suit I demanded to wear at my Bar Mitzvah. It ain't pretty. In fact, the question sucked the soul right out of me. I don't like that mirror held up to my face.

I never responded with a truthful answer, such as, "Dieting makes me lonely and sad," or, "Go fuck yourself, Dad." Instead, I came up with a safe answer—one that both confused folks and bought me some time to retreat, like an octopus spraying ink and heading for the closest hole.

"When I start the diet."

For months, everything hinged on starting the actual diet. Once the diet was under way, all kinds of good things were bound to happen. The unusual marital tension would magically disappear. I'd put down the pâté. I'd stop buying bacon as if it were spinach. I'd start to feel useful again. I might even take a walk. And, if things went really well, there could be more sex again, a rare occurrence since Romy was born.

I can understand why my wife may not want to sleep with me these days. Nothing says sexy like a completely depressed, narcissistic, compulsively eating husband. Whatever was the matter with her?

For a good while now, whatever the question, the answer's always been the same.

"Ed, we're broke."

"When I start the diet . . ."

"Ed, you're fat."

"When I start the diet . . ."

"Ed, you're hiding in the basement."

"When I start the diet . . ."

"Ed, you're obsessing over cooking shows."

"When I start the diet . . ."

"Ed, will you change the baby's diaper?"

"When I start the diet . . ."

The weeks leading up to the start of the project were, well . . . awkward. I was in limbo. I wasn't actually on my health kick. I was all talk. I was still eating as if I were about to spend a month doing a solo on Outward Bound. I was about to board the healthy plane, but eating a lot of things at the gate. I don't know what exactly I was waiting for, but I was sure doing plenty of stalling. Soon enough, I'd actually have to lose all this weight and put my money where my double chin was. How did I handle the pressure? I didn't. I ate everything in sight. It was a dark, dark summer at the Ugel house. (In related news, Ben & Jerry's stock went up two points.)

I'm starting this project with two absolute rules: no fad diets and no pills (except for vitamins). Moreover, I'm going to stop faking it. I'm desperate for help. How do I intend to actually lose the weight? I honestly don't know. What I do know is that I'm the wrong person to make that decision. When left to my own devices, I've never executed a healthy diet and successfully kept the weight off.

A major part of this challenge is to willfully give up control. I'm not the person who should be in charge. I know that I really can't get well without bringing in other people to help. That's true for anyone, no matter what addiction you're fighting. I'm going to listen to the experts this time. A nutritionist is going to tell me how to eat. A trainer will be in charge of my exercise routine. I'm firing myself as CEO of Ed Ugel, Inc. I had the job for a long time and I've basically run the company into the ground. I'm ready to be a loyal foot soldier, a yes-man, a staff-level employee. How am I going to lose this weight and get back into shape? However I'm told.

At this point, even Sasha is wise to what's going on with my health. She may not have the vocabulary to put her dad's girth into words, but she sees what I look like. She's old enough to get it.

For the past three years, Sasha hasn't let me take a shower or even go to the bathroom without keeping me company. Most mornings, when I'm on the toilet, desperate for some privacy, Sasha brings her "work" into the bathroom and sits at my feet coloring or reading while I do my business. If I'm truly lucky, she'll bring her pink Cinderella laptop computer into the bathroom and dance around the toilet to the tune of "It's a Small World (After All)." She has no idea just how small. To the layman, this would seem . . . unnerving. At times, it is. Still, it's kind of our thing now, you know . . . pooping together. We do other stuff, too. It would be odd if this were the only father-daughter bonding ritual we have. Rest assured, it's not. Still, if I'm in the bathroom, odds are so is she. This is something we hope she'll get over before her prom.

When I shower, Sasha always reminds me to close my eyes so the shampoo doesn't sting. It's so damn cute I'm barely bothered by the absolute indignity of it all. Sometimes, when I've had enough, I'll beg her to leave the bathroom. Most days, Sasha will look at me and say, "Daddy, you don't want me to leave." Ironically, when she's not there, part of me does miss her. Such is the life of a parent of young children.

The other day I stepped onto the scale before I got into the shower. It was a big moment, as it was day one of the Fatty Project. I was going to weigh myself and actually write it down.

Sasha came racing through the door, wearing a tiara and waving a magic wand. These days, if she's awake, she's wearing a tiara. I had no tiara, nor magic wand. I had heartburn. Unaware of the gallows march she was interrupting, Sasha waved her wand and turned me into a purple daffodil. I obliged, making a circle with my arms, waving my fingers as if they were petals blowing in the breeze.

I stepped onto the scale and gulped as the digits read 263.4. That's one big daffodil.

"Daddy, how much do you weigh?"

"Two hundred and sixty-three pounds," I said as casually as possible, as if children's fathers the world around were, at that very moment, answering the question the exact same way.

"WOW!" said Sasha. "You're tall."

I then escorted Sasha from the bathroom, went back in, and locked the door for the first time in years.

I weigh an alarming 263 pounds, or as I like to think of it: 119 kilograms. Two hundred and sixty-three pounds is about seventy-five pounds more than I weighed in high school. Seventy-five pounds . . . the size of a nine-year-old boy. A year ago, I weighed 220 pounds, forty-three pounds lighter than I am today. On my wedding day in the spring of 2002, I weighed 253 pounds. I've danced between 213 pounds and 263 pounds for as long as I can remember. Of course, during those rare periods when I've had my weight under control, I was always just a binge or two away from pulling out my fat pants again. My fat pants are never in storage.

This obesity roller-coaster ride runs in my family. All seven members of my immediate family struggle with our weight—even our dog, Maggie, was fat. My folks are still together, still happily married, despite the love-hate, day-to-day grind of raising five kids. The story of my mom and dad's love affair with food (one that I, along with my siblings, inherited at birth) is the story of their forty-three years together.

My folks fell in love while searching for the perfect meal. Today, all these years later—they're still looking. Their first Thanksgiving together began with a forty-mile drive to an old-school butcher my dad had heard about while completing part of his medical residency in Baltimore. When Dad foolishly asked the butcher about the freshness of his birds, the butcher responded by going out back, chasing down, and cutting the head off a screaming, bewildered turkey. He then stripped it of its feathers, gutted it, cut off its feet, threw it in a plastic bag, and handed it to my dad.

"Is that fresh enough for ya, pal?"

"Um, yes. Thank . . . you."

Meekly, my dad handed the butcher some cash, took my mother's hand, and scurried out the door. Mom still talks about that freshly murdered turkey resting against her calf in their tiny blue 1966 Gremlin, the bird's warm flesh giving her the willies the entire trip home. Dinner that Thanksgiving was, nonetheless, a hit.

All the stories that define my family are more than likely edible. These are the stories of our life, told with all the spiciness, aroma, and flavor that food alone gives to memory. A love of food is a tie that binds our family. Many of our best days, our happiest times, our funniest stories, take place at our dinner table, or at any number of restaurants from our childhood. We grew up knowing the produce man at the supermarket, who would keep the best fruit safely tucked away for my mother. We still laugh at the infamous "waffle womping" story at the food court in which the rest of my family attacked my special birthday dessert—finishing it off while I sat there crying. There was the time when my dad ate three Chinese peppers on a bet with my brother and me—just so his two juvenile sons couldn't say he was getting old. Tears, sweat, and snot dripped uncontrollably down Dad's face for the next three hours. They were, perhaps, the happiest three hours of my life.

Growing up, I spent every weekend from Labor Day through Thanksgiving fishing and eating down at the Maryland and Delaware beaches. No matter the weather— wind, rain, even early season snow—come Friday afternoon, Dad, my brother Phil, and I headed to the shore. Spending those fall weekends on the water was a great, privileged way to grow up. We had our beach rituals, little traditions, and inside jokes that now seem so lovely, and so far away.

Phil and I spent our time at the beach split between fishing and hanging out at the boardwalk. We loved the arcades, the rides, and the games offered by the carnival barkers promising stuffed animals, T-shirts, and various other tchotchkes in exchange for whatever cash they could pry out of our hands. While we loved all the amusements, we never strayed too far from the food. In the end, we were there to eat classic beach food: soft-shell crabs, clams and oysters, fried chicken, funnel cakes, frozen custard, Italian and Polish sausages, cheeseburgers, taffy, caramel corn, chocolate licorice, candy apples, cotton candy, and french fries.

Dad would pick us up from school in his 1977 wood-paneled Toyota Corona station wagon, and we'd make the three-hour drive down to the shore. After so many years, I knew those roads, those farms, those endless rows of summer corn and soybeans, better than any stretch of land in the world. I'd watch the sunset in the rearview mirror as the shadows of the telephone poles grew longer and longer, whooshing past, pointing us on our way.

As the fall fishing season progressed, the days got shorter, and the scene at the beach—even the ride down—changed dramatically. The endless sleeping farmlands that separated the city from the shore funneled a stinging fall wind that whipped against our small station wagon, shaking us ever so slightly—taunting us, reminding us of the painful cold waiting for us on the beach at tomorrow's sunrise.

Back in the '70s and early '80s, the beach in late fall was a ghost town. No one was there save for some salty locals and hard-core fishermen crazy enough to brave the elements, all for a chance to catch monster bluefish and rockfish—the last to make their annual run south to warmer waters for the winter. Today, those once-desolate beach roads are now flanked by Home Depots, Cracker Barrels, Bob Evans restaurants, and all the rest of the chains you find anywhere and everywhere. The beach of my youth, like the beach of my father's youth, is gone.

About halfway through our weekly drive to the shore, we'd stop at one of the local fruit stands to pick up some apple cider—maybe a snack, too. Besides fruit and vegetables, the fruit stands sold local baked goods, and fresh roasted peanuts, which sat under a heat lamp to stay warm. On those crisp fall evenings, Phil and I wanted the warm, salty nuts rather than, say, an apple. Dad would often let us buy the peanuts—as long as we pretended to want a few apples as well. Sometimes, he'd even let us pick up a pie or some zucchini bread to "have in the house" for the weekend. "Have in the house" was code for "Don't tell your mom I let you buy this crap when we get back to town."

Dad's main concern was that we not lose our appetites, because within an hour or so, we'd pull into the Rusty Rudder and their All-U-Can-Eat seafood buffet.

The Rusty Rudder was the first major stop on a ritualized weekend foodfest that started Friday night and didn't end until we pulled back into our driveway late Sunday evening. Eating at the Rudder was mayhem—pure chaos. Dad used to joke that they never made money on us because, as kids, Phil and I only paid half price. On paper we were children, but we had very adult appetites. We were both over six feet tall before we turned thirteen.

Dad would eat nothing but seafood from the raw bar the entire meal. Embarrassingly, he'd stack two plates full of raw seafood on top of each other instead of simply eating one plate and then getting up for another. He'd do this awkward balancing act, slowly walking back to the table, trying not to drop the clams and oysters. I'd all but hide under the table when he did that.

Meanwhile, Phil and I weren't exactly shy over at the hot food station. We were pros. We knew what we wanted and what to avoid. Salad? Veggies? Soup? No chance. We were after four things: fried sea scallops, fried shrimp, steamed clams, and steamed snow-crab legs.

Even as I looked on in judgmental horror at my dad's plate-stacking antics, Phil and I mastered the art of piling crab legs a foot high on one plate—you know, classy-like. The trick was to make a base of fried stuff at the bottom and then pile the crab legs on top—wedging the sharp legs into the meaty scallops for support.

The poor waiters couldn't keep up with the mess we made. The second they took away one heaping pile of shells, we'd make another. In the end, all that remained at the table was a mess of tartar sauce, congealing butter, and shards of crab shells. We'd sit there, satiated, picking our teeth with toothpicks fashioned out of the pointy tips of empty crab legs, trying to gin up the energy to get back in the car and drive the last half hour of the trip to Ocean City. For the two hours it took to get to the Rudder, I'd daydream about crab legs and melted butter, my mouth watering like a dog's as we navigated the back roads toward the shore. By the time we finished our meal, I was so full I didn't want to think about food—especially seafood—for at least ten minutes.

As much as food has been an overly large part of my and my family's lives, so have diets. I've started dozens of diets in my life. My family's started more than I can count. When I was growing up, it was pretty obvious when my folks were gearing up for yet another diet. A darkness would descend on the house. The air would change. Tension ruled the day.

How my parents began a diet was largely contingent on my father's mood. If he was happy, a "send-off" in the form of a binge was likely in the cards. If he wasn't, everything from frozen steaks to basic condiments went into the trash. The diet began right then and there—or else.

One good indication that a shotgun diet was on the horizon was when Dad would come home from work in a foul mood and start throwing out unopened jars of mayonnaise and peanut butter. I never understood it—he paid for all that food. It wasn't like he was throwing out ice cream (which he also did). He was throwing out staples— mayo and peanut butter for Christ's sake. Who throws out peanut butter with a house full of five kids? And, if you can't have a mayo jar around without breaking your diet, you've got a whole other set of problems. He'd toss out anything he could find that wasn't healthy, or wasn't physically frozen to the inside of the freezer. Back in the day, that didn't leave a lot of food for us to eat. How much oatmeal can five kids take before they go insane? On the flip side, you've never seen young children have such regular bowel movements.

When my dad hit the wall and decided that his weight was too high to ignore any longer, a diet would start out of nowhere. He'd throw out all our food—and that would be that. Dad just threw out dinner. Okay, guess we're on another diet. Who's excited for black beans and sliced cucumbers with a side of nothing?

Other times, my folks would decide that their diet would begin in say, five days (almost always on a Monday). Once they circled the start date on the calendar, all kinds of unhealthy food would find its way into the house in the days leading up to the diet. It was an odd ritual, the sad countdown to yet another attempt toward a healthier life. Quite possibly the dumbest idea ever to come out of my family, the send-off was, nonetheless, a tradition throughout my childhood. Eating "the good stuff" as fast as you can, as if food were something to sneak in before time ran out, isn't healthy—not physically, and definitely not mentally. At such a young age, seeing food as something to get while you can, before the rules say otherwise, is a setup for a lifetime of failure with food.

Were the send-offs fun? In a way. In the same way an all-night booze bender is fun. But, there are always repercussions. From an early age, I figured out that none of my friend's families had send-offs. It was a Ugel thing—not a Bethesda thing, not a Maryland thing, not a Jewish thing. The send-off was our very own creation. The Mondavis have wine. The Felds have the circus. The Mannings have football. The Fondas all act. And the Ugels . . . we invented the send-off.

Setting aside how ridiculous the idea of a diet send-off was, how insanely unhealthy it was, what a bad example it set for your kids—the send-offs were a time to eat like kings—chubby little kings. During a send-off, nothing was off-limits. It was a free-for-all. But, in the end—it cost us.

Can you imagine anything as detrimental to the start of a reasonable, healthy weight-loss campaign than stuffing yourself full of sugar, carbohydrates, fat, and starch in the days leading up to it? Eating like that and then suddenly stopping and eating nothing but broccoli is asking a lot of your body—not to mention your mind. It almost guarantees failure. I should know. I've been failing at this since I was a kid.

At the end of the day, it's my fault that my weight sky-rocketed over the last few years. No one did this to me. Still, the backstory helps put things in perspective. In early 2006, I was fired from my position as a senior vice president in a finance company that sold up-front cash to lottery winners in exchange for all or some of their future lottery payments. I spent seven years in the "lump sum" business. I excelled at a job that just happened to be in a dark, secretive industry. Leaving, or being asked to leave, after seven years was for the best. But the way the whole thing went down left me with a foul taste in my mouth. Soon thereafter, I decided to write a book about my experiences working with lottery winners.

The company where I worked was none too pleased about the book, and our once strong relationship turned ugly, fast. What followed were several unsuccessful legal challenges from my former employer trying to halt or influence the publication of the book. There were also a few "anonymous" letters sent to my home, trying to scare and intimidate my family. I say "anonymous" because the letters arrived unsigned. The letters were payback for writing my book. It was an ugly, sad time in my life. I was riddled with anger and depression. (And all this before I got my legal bills.) I took comfort in one thing: food.

Now that I was out of a traditional nine-to-five office job, I began taking myself out to lunch nearly every day. I'd go anywhere—to hell and gone—to find new and interesting food. On the way home from my solo lunches, I'd shop for dinner and head home to cook a meal for my family. Food made me happy, or blunted the pains of the day, at a time when my life seemed more and more complicated. When the job, the devoted employees, the corner office, and those big paychecks went away—food was still there for me, as loyal as ever.

Apart from the insane legal headaches, the year I spent writing my first book was great fun. I'd play with my daughter, spend time with Brooke, and I had more time to myself than I'd had since college. I was suddenly a paid writer. I went from working in a depressing, cutthroat industry, to finishing a book in my new basement office, enjoying my life, and washing it down with anything I could eat. The upside? I reported to no one. The downside? I reported to no one.

I had no peers, no colleagues, no boss, no subordinates. I was all alone with my best friend and worst enemy: food. Like a caterpillar tucked away in a buttery cocoon, my body went through a dramatic change over that period of time. I became someone I barely recognized. I went from having a few extra pounds around my belly to a totally different species. I got fat.

Would this excessive weight gain still have happened had I stayed in the business world? When did I actually start to eat like this? Did I start to eat out of depression? Am I an emotional eater? Or do I just love food? That's been a running question in my life for some time now, one that's subjugated my psyche and psychology since I was a kid. I'm riddled with problems. That much I know. I'm just not sure how many of them are caused by food.

Food.

I even like typing the word. F-o-o-d . . . *food. FOOD.* **Food. FOOD.**

This isn't the first time I've gone into battle against my weight. This is, however, the first time I've done so without the assistance of pills.

Several times over the last decade, I took the controversial diet drug Phentermine. Phentermine is half of the infamous weight loss drug cocktail Fen-phen. Yes, I'm referring to *that* Fen-phen . . . the one that helped millions of Americans lose weight until someone dropped dead. For nearly four years, I saw a bariatric doctor who assured me that Phentermine was the "good" part of Fen-Phen, not the "kill you" part. Because he wore a white lab coat, I didn't ask any questions. One all too rarely questions the man who promises you something for nothing.

Did the Phentermine help me lose weight? Absolutely. How can you not lose weight when you're whacked out on what is essentially prescription speed? You're too busy grinding down your teeth to remember to eat. Thanks to my years on Phentermine, my bottom teeth look like those of an Appalachian meth addict.

Phentermine made me so damn jumpy, I used to get spooked when the phone rang or when a waiter approached my table from behind. On the flip side, you sure can get through your to-do list. So remember kids, diet drugs can kill you, but they also make you type faster than Mavis Beacon.

These days, I'm off the pills, but I do spend a good portion of my weekly session with my shrink discussing obesity and body image issues. I'm also known to spend a lot of therapy time—which costs $3 a minute—telling him the best way to slow roast a leg of lamb. This is not good. These aren't the actions of a healthy man. After some sessions, I'm sure my shrink goes home and tells his wife what a nut job I am, but that he's also learned a great new method to sear tuna.

Loving food but being obsessed with my weight, especially my chubby face—is not a winning combination. I'm often too anxious about how I look to enjoy holidays and social functions. No matter the occasion—my wedding day, when my kids were born, my Bar Mitzvah, college graduation; each day was filled with obsessive thoughts about which shirt to wear, whether I could get away with unbuttoning my pants without anyone noticing, or how my chin(s) would look in photos.

What happened to me?

First of all, I never work out—ever. I'll spend all day figuring out a way not to exercise. Brooke comes from a physically active family blessed with fantastic genes. My family can smuggle a large pizza and a couple of gyros into a movie theater without getting caught. So, both sides have a lot going for them.

For the next year, this project means no trips to my favorite dim sum joint every Thursday with Sasha after school. It means no stopping by the Italian store where I get my sweet capicola, mortadella, and roasted peppers on weekends. It means letting go of my five-year obsession with mastering the art of grilling hanger steaks. It means no more pâté, my beloved pâté. It means no more trips to Gifford's ice cream shop, a local institution where I've eaten since I was a kid. It means no idle days spent braising lamb shanks or slow-roasting a pork butt for eight hours, getting the skin crispy, while the fat melts away, just as I learned from my Nana so many years ago. It means changing everything. I might as well change my name.

More than anything else, this project means having to recalibrate my nightly ritual of cooking meals for my family. I'll still make dinner—but it won't be the same. The pleasure of cooking what I want, when I want, will go away—along with the cheeses, the pastas, the butter, and the pancetta. I think I'll miss pancetta the most, my old friend—cured pork. How do I love thee? Let me count the lipids.

I've spent the last few years feeding myself anything and everything—trying to fill a seemingly bottomless hole. Lonely? How about dim sum? Depressed? Carbonara! Legal troubles? That duck dish from the Thai joint by my sister's house. Fighting with the wife? Off to the sushi bar! Writer's block? How about Vietnamese grilled pork and spring rolls? Can't sleep? Ice cream. Feeling like a fat loser? Prove it at McDonald's.

Can someone love food, love eating, and still be able to change his body? Can a foodie get thin again? Can I have my proverbial cake and eat it too? Can you be healthy *and* food obsessed? That's the real question. Can you continue to love food while changing your relationship with it? That's what I'm setting out to answer. Can

I cook interesting, delicious food that's also healthy? Can I live without bacon? What exactly is tofu? Finally, can I—the laziest man I know—actually exercise and re-discover my body again after all these years? Is it too late to see my penis once more without using a mirror? Is that asking too much?

Chapter 3

Imprisoned in every fat man, a thin one is wildly signaling to be let out.

—*Cyril Connolly*

Put me around a wheel of stinky, washed-rind cheese or a pound of good salami and I start twitching like an alcoholic in a dive bar, or a gambling addict walking down Las Vegas Boulevard. I feel surrounded, as if the walls themselves are squeezing the very last ounce of self-control out of me. Lately, I feel like quitting my addiction to food is like ending a love affair. I know it's supposed to hurt, but jeez—this hurts. Right now, my job is to go through the pain.

October is the third in a dozen months where my job, my actual job, is to lose weight, exercise, and start the process of examining my complicated relationship with food. It beats the hell out of washing windows. Yet, I'm not exactly sure I believe that I can lose fifty pounds. It's hard to focus on my new diet in the middle of a Fuddruckers.

Had I gotten off on the right foot and actually started losing weight in September, I wouldn't feel the noose of the holiday season suddenly tightening—even as early as the second week of October.

Despite all my promises not to go on a crash diet, the coming holidays have scared me into action. The first week of October has been a blur of kale, endless glasses of water, carrots, salad greens, poached or grilled chicken breasts, and fruit. I needed to teach my body and my mind a lesson. Santa Claus is coming to town.

The arrival of Halloween is the official beginning of the holiday food gauntlet. Halloween candy acts as a sort of trip wire for the entire holiday season. If you're anything like me, you go nuts with all the candy to the point where you just convince yourself that there's no reason to start or stay on a diet before Thanksgiving gets here, it being only a few weeks away and all. Candy in October always means that I'll eat poorly through the New Year. Only then, in that first week of January, do I start having the same "what have I done to myself" conversation that every other fatty is having with themselves. It's a vicious cycle and it all starts in the candy aisle of the Safeway, the second week of October.

Normally, Brooke tries to buy nothing but hard candy—Starlight mints, butterscotch, cinnamon discs—stuff that holds no interest for either one of us. However, this year—I picked up the candy. Big mistake. It wasn't as if I volunteered. She put it on the shopping list.

I went to the market to pick up a bunch of fruit, salad stuff, and more chicken breasts. I was in a healthy mood. Mr. Salad. The diet king of Bethesda. Overly confident Ed. I felt great walking through the produce aisle, buying stuff

I hadn't eaten in years—if ever. Filling the cart with produce makes you feel good, proud even. Look at me . . . I just bought leeks.

As I made my way from produce to the dairy section, I got a quick dose of reality. Farm fresh chocolate milk? Mooooo. Heavy cream, breakfast sausage, bacon, sugary orange juice, even the yogurt with the fruity syrup on the bottom looked good. Butter! Look, whipped butter! French butter. Salty butter. Crème fraîche? When did they start stocking crème fraîche? I should really try some. . . .

Get out of the grocery store, Ed.

But the girls need cereal, and Brooke told me to get Halloween candy.

Candy? Are you mad? You can't be trusted in the candy aisle.

I'm not a child. Don't talk to me like that.

Okay. My mistake. You are totally in control. The Halloween stuff is on aisle six. Go nuts.

You really don't think I can buy Halloween candy for the neighborhood kids? I'm an adult. I lived in Europe, thank you very much.

So go buy it, then.

I am. Right after I talk to this pint of whipping cream.

Edward!

Okay. Okay. Point made.

Next thing I know, I'm in aisle six tossing bags of mini-Twix, Kit Kats, Snickers, Milky Ways, Almond Joys, and Reese's Peanut Butter Cups into my cart as if I were shopping for myself—which, of course, I was.

I had no business walking down that aisle. I should

have listened to myself. Instead, I'm driving home with a veritable who's who of my favorite candies. I haven't put anything into my mouth yet, but I know how this goes.

It was a huge mistake to buy candy for the trick-or-treaters so far in advance. Consequently, to no one's surprise, I'm on a hell of a candy binge right now. Those little "mini" size bars sure add up. These's nothing mini about *a bag* of minis. It's too damn easy to have just one more. I'm the king of just one more.

I'm angry at Brooke for putting candy on the shopping list and trusting me with this simple errand. I'm not to be trusted in the candy aisle. It's like sending Lennie to go pick up a few mice from the pet store. It never ends well. As a result, I've been walking around the house with a chip on my shoulder because she asked me to "bring poison into the house." I actually had the moxie to say that to her the other day. To her credit, she laughed in my face. Regardless, I've spent the last few days thoroughly blaming her for every single piece of candy I put in my mouth. It's become quite a ritual:

1. Wait for wife to fall asleep.
2. Grab huge handful of candy from Brooke's "secret hiding place."
3. Quietly unwrap all the candy in the kitchen.
4. Make Mars bar and Kit Kat towers on top of a paper towel.
5. Hide surprisingly loud candy wrappers in the bottom of the trashcan.

6. Throw a few unused paper towels on top of trash to act as camouflage.
7. Step on trash with foot to further bury the evidence.
8. Sneak heaping pile of chocolates up to bed.
9. Catch breath.
10. Turn on TV to mask the sound of myself eating a mere nine inches from sleeping wife.
11. Toss individual candies in mouth.
12. Chew.
13. Blame wife for everything that's wrong with me.
14. Repeat.

As a result of all the Halloween candy, October is looking like a rough month. To say the diet has had a "soft opening" would be an insult to soft openings. I just won't stop eating. Since going off the deep end with all the candy, I've been eating basically anything I want for the last few weeks. Some days, I'm actually eating more than I was before I felt the pressure of a diet. That's not good.

Right now there are weeks where I'm gaining weight followed by weeks where I'll lose a pound or two. When I actually lose weight, I get overconfident and celebrate by breaking the diet. It's a bad scene. October, much like September, has been a brutal series of wins and losses. I've yet to figure out the right formula for kicking myself in the ass and staying on track.

Every morning I wake up and promise myself a new

start. But come lunchtime, the little devils in my head start whispering about dumplings and crispy-skinned, roast meats. From there, the battle's almost always lost. It's rare that I stare myself in the eye and say no. That's the hardest thing right now—saying no to myself. I'm realizing that I'm not very good to myself in that way. Just as a good parent will deny their child too many treats, I need to do the same for myself. Kids can't have lollipops every day, and I can't eat chocolate as if it were Shredded Wheat. I know better. I'm allowing myself to be weak. What else is new?

The one bit of good news is that I just joined yet another health club. But inevitably, after going through the indignity of waddling in and joining, I never go back. I'm sure they're shocked. A fat guy joined the club and never returned. How cliché.

You never feel fatter than while walking into the lobby of a health club for the first time in years. It's like an intervention staged by perfect strangers. You feel guilty the second you enter. I wanted to go around apologizing to everyone for everything I've ever eaten. The health club intimidated the hell out of me. Even the old people looked better than me.

The actual process of joining a health club is a needlessly painstaking, personally invasive procedure. I felt like I was being audited. You can't just walk in and hand over your credit card. They make you talk to a extremely irritating salesperson who's working off a scripted pitch. My saleswoman, Judy, is just overcome with pep and energy. She can't wait to tell me how great I'm going to feel as soon as I take advantage of their one-time free personal-training consultation. Well, goody for me.

Judy is not the leggy brunette that Ross and Chandler dealt with when Chandler wanted to quit the gym on *Friends*. No such luck. My gatekeeper to the gym is the single happiest, most caffeinated, gung-ho saleswoman I've ever come across. She's just so damn excited that I'm joining the gym, I think her eyes are going to pop out of their sockets. Not even Brooke is this excited that I'm joining. Sasha was less intense at the circus last spring.

"Do you have your own trainer now?!" she asks nearly jumping onto her desk. She's trying to pitch me a "deluxe" membership, which I'm as likely to purchase as I am a llama farm. My insides burn with frustration. I'm also getting kind of humiliated. *Do I fucking look like I have my own trainer?* She's just about the worst salesperson I've ever met—which is saying something. I want to help her sell me by telling her to stop talking. I'm a sure thing. I'm here to buy. Do you think I'd be here if I weren't going to sign up? We can close this deal right now and both go home. Stop talking. I have my credit card in my hand.

"I think you know the answer to that," I say without looking up from the brochure.

"One never knows!!" she cheerfully adds. She's so goddamn perky and fit and tan. I hate her.

"Oh, I'm pretty sure 'one knows' in this case. One just has to look at the customer and figure that out all by one's self. One needn't ask questions to which they already know the answer."

"I see . . ." she says, gasping for air as if I just punched her in the gut.

I've upset her. I instantly feel like a bully. Ashamed of myself, I throw her a bone and do my best to act like I'm interested in hearing more about their personal trainers.

"How much are your trainers anyway? Do they charge by the hour?"

She comes right back to life and answers, but I'm not listening. Frankly, I just don't care. I'm barely holding on. I'm one stupid question away from either throwing her desk out the window, or having a panic attack. Either way—I've tuned out. I sign my contract and toss my credit card on the desk.

"Can you run this while I use the restroom?" I ask.

"Don't you want the full tour? We have a new Pilates studio," she pleads.

I just stare at her until it's absolutely clear that, in fact, I do not want the tour. I want to pretend to use the bathroom so I can get out of her suffocating office while she finishes up the paperwork.

"Why don't I just run this so you can be on your way?" she whispers as if finally realizing that there is no Easter Bunny. She gets it. I'm a portly monster. I don't want to pretend that I'm happy to be here. That's her job.

"Great! Thanks so much!" I do my best to smile in a way that doesn't make me look insane. Unfortunately, I have a sneaking suspicion that ship has sailed.

I came into old Judy's office with more emotional baggage than most folks she'll see on an average Monday. She's intolerable, but I'm being an ass. When I'm embarrassed, I get like that. And, boy, am I embarrassed. It's not her fault that I can barely fit into her chair. It's not her fault that the health club forces her to up-sell the personal-trainer package. She's just doing her job. Coincidentally, I'm here trying to do mine.

If I'm going to make a real effort to get healthy, I've got to find a way to feel comfortable at the health club. Right now, it's a toss-up between where I'd feel less at home for the next year—the gym or a Miley Cyrus concert. I'm so entirely out of shape, starting to exercise feels like a fruitless endeavor—like setting out to count all the sand at the beach. Where do you start? No matter how well-intentioned I may be, am I really going to stick with it? After nearly two decades, am I suddenly going to become a gym guy? Am I fooling myself? I've joined health clubs several times over the last decade. I even went a time or two. But in the end, I never stuck with it long enough to see any results. It only made my body ache a few times before I gave up on myself. This time, things have got to be different. I know I can't do it alone. Beyond joining the club, I've got to find myself a trainer and a nutritionist, fast.

After a few good weeks of healthy living, I went on the inexplicable eating binge. What caused me to fall apart? I wish I had some dramatic excuse. I do not. Indeed, I was already feeling the effects of my good behavior of the preceding few weeks. After dropping three or four pounds, there was already a difference in my face—normally the first place I gain and lose weight. For the first time in forever, I felt like I was on my way.

I have no excuse for the breakdown. The Good Humor ice cream truck never pulled into my driveway and refused to leave until I ate everything that wasn't bolted to the floor. However, something happened which surely didn't help. Brooke went out of town to a conference for five days, leaving me alone with the girls.

I love spending time alone with my kids. There is nothing better than being their dad. Plus, you get a different payoff when their mom isn't around for them to go to when they need help, love, food, diapers, rides, Kleenex, kisses, medicine, or tickles. I'm the only game in town when Mommy's gone. Thus, the Daddy Show is standing room only. They can't get enough of me. In Brooke's absence I get more than my share of love from the girls. Still, I just can't help it—I miss Brooke.

When Brooke's out of town, I act out in the strangest ways. I get lonely without her here. I miss the stupidest things, like watching *Survivor* and betting on who'll be voted off the island or fighting over the pillows. I miss her maddening, incessant reminders about what time I need to pick up Sasha from school or exactly which day the trash cans need to go to the curb. The fact that I've been picking Sasha up from school for the last three years without once forgetting her there and forcing her to sleep in the gym, or that the trash has been picked up on the same day every week since we bought this house seven years ago doesn't stop her from reminding me. It drives me crazy that she treats me as if I were a child. The fact that she's right doesn't negate the point. I am a child. I'm spoiled. I'm lazy. I forget everything the second it's told to me. I pout at the drop of a hat. I get cranky when I'm tired. I always want my way. I occasionally wet my bed. Still, how dare she.

This time around, when Brooke left town, I turned to my old outlet—food.

I had help during the day. My mother-in-law, Karen, came over to take care of Sasha and Romy while Brooke was traveling. I really only had to take care of the kids by myself in the evenings. Unfortunately, it was during the daytime, when I was alone, that things fell apart.

The plan was for me to exercise and work during the day. That's why Karen agreed to step in and help. Things started off pretty well. I was either working out on the cardio machines at the gym or going for long walks on the Capital Crescent Trail, which cuts through the heart of Bethesda. Walking through the local forest a few times doesn't exactly make me an outdoorsman, but it was a monumental upgrade from what I'd been doing this time last year. During my recent outings, I was power walking, listening to my iPod, and pretending to enjoy myself on some of Bethesda's most beautiful stretches of land. By the time I'd make it back to my car, I'd be dripping with sweat. I enjoyed looking like someone who exercised. It was a nice change. Once I finally went to the Sports Authority and bought some compression shorts, even my terrible case of Mr. Chaffey started to go away. (Mr. Chaffey is my family's term for what happens when your inner thighs rub together, causing great discomfort and a propensity to walk like a penguin.)

After my walks on the trail, I'd crawl into my car and

go directly home for a salad or some lean protein—maybe some chicken breast with grilled veggies. I'd sit in my kitchen detailing my adventures to Karen as if I were Odysseus back from the wars. For the first time in forever, I was proud of myself. The salads and veggies weren't exactly what I was in the mood for, but I was finally getting into the whole healthy living scene. I ate healthy. I acted healthy. I felt healthy.

Then the wheels came off the bus.

The day Brooke left town, I took my walk just as I'd been doing. I made my way back to the parking lot—but walked right past my car. I walked directly to Shanghai Village, our local Chinese restaurant, and ordered Crispy Beef and two egg rolls to go. I walked back to my car, drove the two blocks back to the restaurant, and picked up my food. Knowing that Karen was at the house with the girls, I wouldn't dare go there with a bag full of fried Chinese food. I might have to share it. Instead, I drove into the closest neighborhood, found a secluded spot, and ate the whole meal out of the containers, right there in the car.

It was as if someone else had control of my brain. I didn't even want the food. Every bite tasted like failure. I sat there parked in front of someone's house, binging on the usual crap—same old Edward. I could pretend that I'd changed but, deep down inside, I knew better. This is who I am, who I've become. I'm a fat old dog. There are no new tricks.

Once I fell, I fell hard.

Over the next five days, during the day, I'd pretend

that I was headed to the library or to the walking trail, only to eat my way through town. I didn't just break the diet, I shattered it. All week long, come lunch time, I'd get my familiar hankering for Asian food. In five days, I had dim sum, Korean barbecue, Malaysian, and Thai food. I also ate ice cream every day—smuggling it into my office through the basement door so Karen wouldn't see it. It doesn't get more depressing than sneaking food into your own house.

When I want to eat without being seen, I head to the fringes of the city, where I'm less likely to bump into anyone I know. Anonymous shame. I bring a book and go to little out-of-the-way places that Brooke never wants to try nearly as much as I do. I grew up in a family that thought nothing of driving an hour to try a new restaurant. Brooke did not. She sees driving a half hour just to eat as the act of a madman. Throughout my childhood, these little adventures were always great fun. These days, a trip to a random restaurant gives me something to do when I get cabin fever and decide to leap off the diet wagon.

While Brooke was away, I went to a restaurant called Ruan Thai three times. Ruan Thai is the kind of tiny, hole-in-the-wall joint that I'm drawn to. Plus, being on the other side of town, it's a perfect hideaway for my bender. They make the best duck dish I've ever had. I've had it twenty times over the past year, or six months . . . or three. It's a wok-fried sliced duck breast with basil, peppers, and hot chilies. When the kitchen is on its game, the fat from the skin gets rendered, leaving behind nothing but perfectly crisp skin. (Imagine a duck-flavored potato chip.) The meat itself is fork tender, falling apart as if braised for hours. The complementary textures of the crispy skin and the tender breast meat holds up against the Thai chilies. It's the perfect dish—at least this week's perfect dish.

Looking back, I've tried to figure out if there was a trigger, a moment where the road split, where I could have avoided this train wreck of a week. What would have happened if I'd just had a salad at home that day after my walk? Would the week have been salvaged? Perhaps. Sadly, I also think that somewhere in my mind, I was waiting for Brooke to leave so the levee could break. I think a little bit of success was getting to me. Staying on track over the course of a few weeks gave me a sense of entitlement to reward myself. I hadn't eaten this well in forever. It was as if I knew I wasn't going to keep it up— so why not fail now?

For these twelve months, being healthy is my job. Would I sabotage myself like this in an office full of coworkers? It's unlikely. So why did I just knock over the cards I've been stacking? What is it about the slightest hint of success that makes me head for the hills? Is it just the way I do things? Is it because I wanted fattening food so badly? Is food that powerful in my life or did I just need an excuse to get out of the house and act badly?

I get a little nutty spending my days and nights at home surrounded by no one other than my wife and daughters. I write from my home office. I also happen to live at home—meaning I spend a lot of time here. Lately, I'm even more inclined to stay home because I've gained so much weight. I don't want to bump into someone I know and have to talk to them while I'm just overflowing with girth and shame. Add all my little idiosyncrasies and fears together and you've got yourself a man just shy of being a shut-in.

The five days without Brooke were a disaster. I gained back most of the weight I'd lost so far. The daily walks on the trail? Not once. The gym? Nope.

When Brooke came home, I told her everything—or almost everything. She needn't know I was smuggling ice cream into the basement freezer. Brooke and I agreed on one thing. It was well past time for me to get out of the house and find myself a trainer. Enough of the long walks through the forest. It was time to put my exercise routine in someone else's hands.

Short of opening up the Yellow Pages, or doing a Google search, I didn't know where to begin. Where's the best corned beef in town? Need a good bakery? A raw bar? How about an honest car mechanic? I'm your guy. However, when it came to finding a trainer in DC, I'm from out of town. What in the world do I know about trainers?

Who did I ask for guidance? Brooke's ninety-four-year-old grandmother.

Edith Bralove has been a part of Washington, DC, society life since the Truman administration. She knows everybody and *everybody* knows her. She's a patron of the arts, a Democrat, a wine lover—good people by all accounts. She has a beautiful home in Georgetown with a postcard-worthy view of the city and the Potomac River.

Edie's a petite woman but a presence in any room. She doesn't suffer fools, and it practically says "fool" on my business card. Therefore, my reliance on fart jokes or the use of the term "dude" gets shelved while in her company. She's a lady, and I do my best to act like a gentleman when she's around. Still, she's no porcelain doll. She's funny and knows how to have a good time.

Edie's as independent as Miss Daisy and stubborn as a mule when it comes to protecting her sovereignty. She drives a black Volkswagen Beetle and will have her license taken away only when someone has the balls to try to pry it out of her hands. I, for one, do not.

Stunningly, she works out with a trainer three or four days a week. She's done so for nearly twenty years. The only thing I've done nearly every day for twenty years is attempt to have a healthy bowel movement. Recently, I found myself sitting with her at my nephew's birthday party. I told her I wanted to call her trainer, David Keller, to pick his brain about the best way to lose all this weight.

Edie put us together the following day.

I wasn't planning on using David as my trainer. It was too close to home. After so many years of working together, David and Edie have become friends and companions. They attend theater and gallery shows. At times, they even travel together. Sharing my ninety-four-year-old grandmother-in-law's trainer wasn't how I saw myself getting back into fighting shape. Still, from the little I knew of him, he'd be a good source to find *my* trainer. Calling him was important. No matter who he was, calling him meant crossing a line. I was finally putting this trainer thing in motion instead of just talking about it.

David is one of those rare people without a lot of baggage, without games, without so many of the social malfunctions that riddle me. He's remarkably handsome. He is fifty-three years old, six-foot-five, perfectly fit, tanned, and muscular. Imagine a blond, gay Clark Kent in oversize tortoiseshell glasses.

I met David nearly a decade ago when Brooke and I lived in Manhattan. He and his partner were in New York for the weekend. We bumped into the two of them coming around a corner on the Upper West Side. David warmly shook my hand in his massive paw, and I had to stop myself from staring at him when he asked me a question. I just couldn't take my eyes off the guy. He looked as I imagined Thor would look in real life.

David was expecting my call. He'd already heard the details of my project from Edie. And to my surprise, he remembered our brief meeting in the city. After a thirty-second explanation about what I was doing, David cut me off in mid-pitch. "I'm the one you're looking for," he said. "Come to my studio tomorrow morning."

"But David, I'm just—"

"Just be here tomorrow. Say ten o'clock?"

"Well, I was only sort of looking to just talk, you know?"

"We'll talk tomorrow. That way, I can get a good look at you and see what we're dealing with."

"It ain't pretty."

"It never is."

"I don't know that I'm actually ready to start. I was just sort of kicking—"

"Kicking tires?"

"Yeah, just looking around for the best fit."

"When did you start this health regimen?"

"August."

"How much weight did you lose in August?"

"I gained ten pounds . . ."

". . . See you in the morning."

"I'm broke."

"I've heard."

"I'm lazy."

"Heard that too."

"I'm scared of you."

"Get in line."

Our call lasted three minutes. Despite my intentions going in, it seemed I'd found my trainer. How do you say no to Superman?

Until that morning, I'd never intentionally been within fifty feet of a trainer, as they tend to hang out in places like health clubs or juice bars, and I have a propensity for slow walks through food courts. In my mind, a trainer wore spandex shorts, a tight T-shirt, and was known to say things like "feel the burn." I always thought of trainers the same way I thought of palm readers—fine for some folks, just not me.

David made a tidy sum investing in residential and commercial real estate in the '90s. Although he's lived in Georgetown for decades, the last dozen years have found him bouncing from town house to town house, renovating and flipping properties along the way. David had recently bought a town house kitty-corner to public tennis courts and two blocks from a park on a beautiful street in a sought-after neighborhood. He's turned the first two floors of the four-level property into an exercise studio where he sees clients. The two top floors are his living space.

For months, I had dreaded the idea of going to a real health club and exercising in front of strangers, or worse—someone I knew. David's private studio was the perfect solution. His house was an oasis, a place where I could relearn how to exercise without the indignity of doing it in public. Granted, I needed to go to the gym to lift weights and whatever else they do there. I needed to face the stress and insecurities waiting for me at the gym—just not yet. After so many years of doing nothing, lifting weights at the gym was more than I cared to tackle right now. At David's studio, I could avoid the psychologically loaded scene at the gym, at least for a little while.

The drive to his house that crisp fall morning was a real low point for me. I'd been spending all my time in a mirrorless basement office. I'd go out with Brooke, the kids, or friends, but I wasn't doing a heck of a lot of playing with others those days. Whenever possible, I was at home. To comfortably go out of the house requires confidence, interest, and a pair of pants that you can button without cutting off circulation to your testicles. I was lacking on all fronts.

My desire to stay away from people had been growing like summer weeds in tandem with my weight gain over the past year. David was about to take on a monster, a food-addicted, out of control, sociopathic glutton. I'd been doing little else besides eating my way through this sad, desperate phase of my life. I was hoping that someone, anyone, could step in and save me. I was lost.

Enter David—cape and all.

David opened the door in what I'd soon come to know as his daily uniform: khaki shorts and a white polo shirt . . . collar up, of course. He looked like a model for the East Hampton set. Like his house, he was immaculately kept, perfectly groomed. I hadn't shaved in a week. His hair was full of product. I wore a Redskins baseball cap, because I hadn't showered. I figured showering before you meet with a trainer was like eating before you go to cooking class.

David sat me down and, to my surprise, immediately offered me coffee. He was human. I was reticent about accepting. Was this a test, offering the fat guy coffee? What was I supposed to say? Yes? No? I was so nervous, I didn't even know how to accept a cup of coffee. I really wanted one. I always want coffee.

"No. I'm fine, thanks."

David looked at me as if I was lying—which I was. "You drink coffee, don't you?"

"Religiously."

"Then have a cup. It's Starbucks, and I brew it better than they do. How do you take it?"

"Black, with just a bit of sweetener."

"Sugar?"

"Sure." I couldn't believe he offered me sugar. I was going to lie and say Splenda, but why bother? How I take my coffee was the least of my—our—problems.

He disappeared and returned with a cup for each of us. I'm here for two minutes and he's giving me sugar and caffeine. Interesting. I half hoped he'd put out a tray of crullers. No dice.

He swore that he could help me—even though I knew that I was beyond help. He went on these wild tangents about our unhealthy culture, kayaking, the exercise industry, his philosophy on fitness, dogs, music, and why the food we eat is making our population feel so sick all the time. He also seemed intent on convincing me that he too was a food lover, a cook even. Wow, a cook! I couldn't have cared less. Just what I needed, another cook in my life. I know he was trying to relate to me—this thing that showed up at his door—but I didn't really care that he liked food. I didn't care that he liked movies or kayaking or men or Edie or puppies. All I could think was that I'd made a huge mistake. He was putting his claws into me and I could tell he wasn't planning on letting go. I nervously sipped my coffee, nodding my head in agreement with everything he said.

Next came his health questionnaire. I can only imagine that he cut it short after the first few answers. "There's no right or wrong answer," he said. "So just do your best and be as candid as possible."

"Of course." I said. As if I, the moron who grudgingly showed up for this appointment, now drinking a

big sugary cup of coffee, would ever dream of lying. Moi?
Lie? About my weight? About my, ahem . . . weekly exercise level? Whatever would I do that for?

"What's your current level of exercise?" he asked.

"You mean daily? Weekly? Monthly?"

"Daily . . ."

"None."

"Okay. How 'bout weekly?"

"Um . . . none."

"Monthly?"

"Which month? Any in particular?"

"This month?"

"None."

"Last month?"

"A lot like this month."

"When's the last time you did any regular exercise?"

"How far back does your calendar go?"

"Seriously. When was the last time you got a good sweat going?"

"Does sex count?"

"Absolutely!"

"It's still been a few years—like ten, maybe."

"Do you miss it?"

"What, sweaty sex?"

"No. Being physically active?"

"I haven't really thought about it. It's been so long.
I think I miss it. I used to be an athlete."

"What happened?" he asked.

"Not sure . . . college? Girls? Back surgery? Studying?

Jobs? Food? I really can't say. And, whatever I say doesn't really matter, right?"

"You're right. I just wonder if you miss being in better shape."

"Do I miss it? Of course. It just feels very far away. Like Siberia, you know?"

"You ready to start?"

"Not as ready as I thought I'd be."

"We're going to start real slow, I promise."

"How's next summer?"

"How's right now?"

"You want to start *now* now?"

"I sure do."

And we did. We started right then and there. It wasn't hard. It was humiliating. But it wasn't hard. All I did for the rest of the session was stand in front of a full length mirror. That's it. We just looked at my body.

Ever try that? Ever really look at yourself?

I hadn't looked at my body in years. What's to look at? Why do it to yourself? I haven't looked in any Dumpsters either. Who needs the grief?

It was really something, just standing there while David talked to me about each section of my body. He taught me to look at my body as a series of blocks—each one's stability necessary to keep the rest of me aligned and healthy. That's when I learned that my posture (think somewhere between a gorilla and Big Pussy from *The Sopranos*) was bad because my lower back was overcompensating for my weak shoulders. Apparently, I also suffer from standing like a little pigeon-toed girl. And here I just thought I was fat.

There was some good news. David told me, over and over again, that I was strong, that I was naturally muscular, that under all this fat was a big solid frame, able to build and grow muscle quicker than most. Jealous? He wasn't just giving me the company line—telling me the same thing everyone else hears when they stumble through his door. Apparently, I was different. I was even lucky to have a "mesomorphic" body, meaning that I can lose weight and add muscle faster than most other folks. Basically, I'm like a superhero.

A mesomorphic body type is one with well-defined muscles on the trunk and limbs. Mesomorphs are broad in the shoulders and hips. He actually used the word "lucky" to describe my body. I didn't feel lucky. Was it my man boobs that made me lucky? My round face? The spare tire anchoring my belly? My sumo wrestler's thighs that chafed and got sore whenever I wore shorts? If I was lucky, I wanted to meet one of the unlucky ones . . . the ones with the bad bodies. When did I get to meet them? What did they hear when they stood in front of David's magic mirror?

Not only did he start fitting me into his schedule, he refused to hear that I was too busy to come and exercise with him nearly every day. It was that simple. Ever since we met, I've stopped listening to myself and started listening to him. I'm eating what David tells me to eat. I run till he says stop. I lift the weights that he puts in my hands. Five more push-ups? Yes, David. Ten more minutes on the elliptical machine? Yes, David. Can I be here at 8 AM tomorrow? Yes, David. Drink this chalky protein shake? Yes, David. David is now in control of my life. I've willingly given him the power to tell me what to do. He's my Jim Jones, without the Kool-Aid and with much better hair.

I wasn't doing much of a job taking care of myself, so I outsourced the work to someone better qualified. It's a hell of a thing giving that kind of control to another person. It was both cathartic and unnerving letting him take charge. I'd spent the last twenty years doing nothing healthy. Now, I had a serious, committed routine. It was wonderful. I also hated every minute of it.

There was a lesson there, even that early in the game. Whoever you are, wherever you live, whatever your financial situation—go find your own David Keller. If you can't afford a personal trainer, join a group. If you live in the middle of nowhere, train with someone online. If you just don't have the time, stop bullshitting yourself. Make the time. Without a David Keller in your life, getting healthy is going to be a long, lonely, nearly impossible gig to pull off.

Chapter 4

And if you gaze for long into an abyss, the abyss gazes also into you.

—*Friedrich Nietzsche*

THE HOLIDAY PLAN

1. Exercise five days a week. Okay—four or five days a week, but definitely four.
2. Document all meals in a daily food journal.
3. Eat a real breakfast every morning (egg whites, fruit, chicken sausage, smoked fish, veggies).
4. Stay away from white food (sugar, pasta, bread . . . buttercream icing).
5. Resist urge to choke Santa at mall. It's not his fault that you smell Cinnabon and can't have it.
6. Cancel plan to make Hanukkah menorah out of Krispy Kreme doughnuts.

Ho-ho, woe.

The holiday season is not my best time of the year. I'm really no good at parties—especially not these days. I just don't feel comfortable in my own skin. This year, we have a few holiday things—not as many as Brooke would like, but more than I prefer.

Brooke describes my emotional and psychological take on the holidays as resting somewhere between bah, humbug, and antisocial whack job. I could argue the point, but, well—she's right.

It's not as if we're invited to dozens of holiday parties, anyway. Frankly, we're not that popular. I'm likely to blame for that—charmer that I am. Plus, neither Brooke nor I work for a company anymore. We are both self-employed. Thus, I gleefully avoid two excruciating holiday parties just by the nature of our current state of employment. I used to dread my old company's holiday party. Between making small talk with my staff's spouses and making sure none of my direct reports drank too much and threw up on the buffet, it was a gig I'd have been happy to avoid.

This holiday season, in addition to my traditional stocking full of social anxiety, I'm knee deep in the Fatty Project. If there was ever a holiday season to keep it together, it's this one. But I'm not exactly on diet cruise control just yet. I know myself too well to think that I'm going to eat like a rabbit on Thanksgiving. I'm going to eat a full Thanksgiving dinner. I just am. But, Thanksgiving dinner isn't where things get dicey for me. It's all the days leading up to that dinner, not to mention the no-man's-land in the weeks between Thanksgiving and New Year's.

At this point, I'm just trying to get through it without ruining what little progress I've made thus far. Losing weight in the next two months? It just doesn't seem possible.

The actual holidays themselves are just a few days. Whatever you eat at Thanksgiving, Christmas, Hanukkah, Kwanzaa, or New Year's Eve isn't going to make that big of a difference to your overall health. But, tie together three to eight weeks of a devil-may-care holiday mind-set, and you're really looking at a year-changing equation.

There's no avoiding the handful of parties and family dinners we'll be attending in the next eight weeks. But my body simply can't survive two months of chaos. I've got to find a way to manage the holidays.

Looking back, now that the holidays are nearly over, I'm thrilled with the results. I've lost nearly eleven pounds over the months of November and December. Suck it, Dick Clark.

I was able to follow my exercise plan. I actually played racquetball nearly every day for the entire eight holiday weeks. Right now, I'm so hooked on playing, it hardly feels like a workout. I've found something healthy that I love to do. The whole dynamic of the project has changed.

I've also been keeping a daily food journal, which is a huge pain in the ass. At first, I wasn't completely honest about what I ate. I'd omit a handful of animal crackers, that last string cheese just before bed, or the three 1-point Weight Watchers ice cream bars I shoved in my mouth while Brooke was reading in the next room. Finally, in early November, I started writing *every-thing* down.

If you're anything like me, you've grown accustomed to hurting yourself in one way or another. It's humbling to look back over a week or a month and see everything you ate. If you're honest with your food journal, it highlights some nasty truths about your eating habits. Finally being honest about what I was eating has been surprisingly liberating.

Here are the first honest food journal entries from the first week of November.

Monday, November 3

- Breakfast: 1 cup of coffee with Splenda, 1 Dannon peach (fruit on the bottom) yogurt

- Lunch: Egg salad on wheat toast, 3 oz. pita chips, Coke Zero

- Snack: Cashew granola bar

- Dinner: 2 slices of pizza, salad with Italian dressing, 1 red wine, 1 vodka soda

- Midnight Snack: Handful of cashews

Tuesday, November 4

- Breakfast: 1 cup of coffee with Splenda, 1 Dannon peach (fruit on the bottom) yogurt

- Snack: 2 oz. semisoft cheese (brie)

- Lunch: 1 hot dog with mustard, 6–7 french fries, Coke Zero

- Snack: Cashew granola bar

- Dinner: 3–4 carrot sticks with hummus, steamed broccoli, steamed yellow squash, plain whole wheat pasta, 2 slices avocado, 2 glasses red wine (We were invited to dinner at a vegan household. Miserable.)

- Midnight Snack: 5 oz. yogurt raisins

Wednesday, November 5
- Breakfast: 1 cup of coffee with Splenda, 1 Dannon strawberry (fruit on the bottom) yogurt

- Lunch: Chicken salad on wheat toast, small bag pretzels, Coke Zero

- Snack: Cashew granola bar

- Dinner: Sushi (6 pieces crunchy shrimp roll, 6 pieces spicy tuna roll, 2 raw scallops, tuna tartare)

- Midnight Snack: Handful of cashews, cashew granola bar

After writing down my entire food intake for a few days, there were obviously some areas that needed attention. For example, what led me to believe that I could eat all those cashews? I'd never looked into the fat or calories in cashews. I just assumed they were healthy, or healthy enough. And what about my newly developed granola bar habit? Granola's okay, right? And all the yogurt? I can eat all the yogurt I want, can't I?

Here are a few facts about my "healthy" eating from the beginning of November.

1) Cashews are loaded with fat. One ounce of raw cashews has 155 calories and 103 calories from fat. If you're eating salted cashews, which you undoubtedly are, the calories go up to 160, the calories from fat rise to 117 grams—not to mention 110 mg of sodium. And, honestly, who's really just eating 1 ounce of nuts? Not me. When I'm eating cashews, I'll likely eat closer to four or five ounces. Suddenly, those "healthy" nuts are adding roughly 800 calories and 500 calories from fat to your day. Final analysis: Enough with the cashews.

2) Cashew granola bars are nearly as caloric as an ice cream bar. They have 160 calories, 117 calories from fat. A Hershey bar has 210 calories and 110 calories from fat. A Good Humor Chocolate Éclair ice cream bar has 160 calories and 70 calories from fat. It's actually less fattening to eat a Good Humor ice cream bar than a cashew granola bar. *Huh?* Yes, this meant that during the previous two months I could have had sixty chocolate éclair bars instead of all those goddamn granola bars. Final analysis: Granola bars are not nearly as healthy as you think. In fact, many are com-

parable to eating a chocolate bar, which is a lot more fun.

3) Yogurt is basically fruit pudding. There are 150 calories per cup and 15 fat calories. Not bad, right? But I was stunned to learn that a Dannon Fruit on the Bottom style yogurt has 26 grams of sugar per cup. To put that in perspective, a packet of sugar has 4 grams of sugar. Therefore, every cup of yogurt you eat has the equivalent of 6.5 packets of sugar in it. Can you imagine putting 6.5 packets of sugar in your coffee? Final analysis: If you're going to eat fruit yogurt, you might as well eat a scoop of ice cream. They both have 26 grams of sugar inside.

In the end, you've got to read the labels. Sadly, you must also be defensive when you shop. Assume that companies are hiding calories and all kinds of things they'd rather you not see. The more ingredients, the more suspicious you should be.

One night just before New Years, I was asleep with the CPAP mask shoved up my nose as prescribed by Dr. Williams. I'd only recently been able to fall asleep with the mask on without feeling the urge to rip out my hair. Sadly, I'd been growing somewhat used to it. At about 2:30 AM, Sasha stumbled into our room to use the bathroom. Next thing I know, I'm jolted awake by Sasha standing next to my head, pointing at me, and screaming like that little girl in *Poltergeist*. I think her exact words were, "Something's wrong with Daddy!" Truer words have never been spoken.

That's an unnerving phrase to hear at any time of day, especially when you're the daddy in question. At 2:30 AM, all bets are off as to what it could mean. Coward that I am, I was instantly as scared as her. I briefly considered using her as a shield or peace offering to whatever six-eyed monster had made its way into our house.

In a panic, I jumped up and started looking all over the room for whatever she saw. Was it a snake? Had I been stabbed? Did my water just break? Once I gained my composure, I realized that Sasha was referring to the alienesque CPAP mask seemingly heading for my brain via my nostrils.

We hadn't really explained the whole CPAP mask to Sasha figuring that she was just too young to understand or care. In hindsight, it would have been a whole lot easier, and more humane, had we thought this whole thing through.

Brooke had to calm us both down.

By the time we got Sasha back to sleep, it was nearly 3:30 AM. This just can't be for the rest of my life.

No matter how much I hate the CPAP mask, I've got to admit that I've been sleeping better. Brooke concurs. Perhaps because I'm more rested, I'm not dreading the exercise as much as I did just a short time ago.

I've been exercising consistently, in one form or another, since I met David. I either work out at his studio or play racquetball nearly every day. I've only just begun to lose weight, but I'm already healthier than I've been in twenty years. I'm moving my body again. I'm happier. I'm not nearly as depressed as I was last summer. The exercise is a big change. Before this, the only time I'd gotten my heart rate up over the last two decades was when the elevator was out at my old job.

For November, December, and January, the exercise side of the project's gotten an A–. The weight-loss side bounces between a D+, painfully reminiscent of my high school algebra days, and a solid B. Sadly, there's no summer school option available this time around. Even though I have a good amount of weight left to lose, I've surprised myself when it comes to exercising. I'm working out. I lift weights. I do that goofy thing where I thrust my chin up to say hello when I see someone I recognize at the gym. I'm sort of cool in there now. In fact, I'm there so much that I've actually started to understand the odd dynamics of health club culture. I've grown to hate the jerks who sit around naked in the locker room, spewing their theories about the recession and why Obama's ruining the country.

When did health club locker rooms become the new hang-out spot for rich, old men? It's like an old-timey soda fountain in there. Where are all the young people milling about snapping rat-tails into each other's calves? They sure as hell aren't in this one. My steam room overflows with alter cockers hell-bent on ruining my schvitz time making sure everyone knows that *they* pulled their money out of the stock market just before it crashed. Well, I didn't, and you're desperately in need of a Brazilian wax. Please cross your legs.

Still, if you'd told me three months before that my biggest problem at the club would be geezers with their dicks hanging out, I'd have hugged you. A year ago, I was too heavy to walk up a flight of stairs without getting winded. I hadn't lifted a weight, nor walked a mile, in years—much less enjoyed a workout. The old farts at the club gave me something to laugh about while I was on the elliptical or the StairMaster. When I was huffing and puffing away, they took my mind off the monotony of what I was doing. The fact that I could breathe again, that I had recently touched my toes for the first time since the Clinton administration, trumped some annoying old dude's take on politics—but just barely.

I love sweating. Who knew? I'd forgotten how much I love it. Yet, despite my success on the exercise front—I was still eating like a fat guy. Exercise helps, but it doesn't give you a license to eat like you're spending your last evening on death row. I'd been pretending that the good I was doing exercising was trumping the bad decisions I was making about food. It wasn't. At best, it was a draw.

Control's a funny thing. It comes and goes. Some days I had it, some days I didn't. It felt like every time I did something healthy, I had this insatiable need to counterbalance it by doing something unhealthy. But that winter, just when I'd gone off the deep end, I was able to step away from the cliff's edge and pull myself together. When you look at this pattern from a macro level, it means I was rarely actually gaining any ground. I was basically just gaining and losing the same few pounds over and over again. It was incredibly frustrating.

Some days, I'd leave David's studio and quickly drive somewhere to eat. It was almost like it was happening to someone else, like the conscious me would never do this to myself. Some days, I'd drive directly to the Tackle Box, a New England–style fried-fish joint, for a plate of fried clams and french fries. Other days, I'd stop at this falafel shop a few blocks from David's place and eat a steak and cheese . . . with a side of falafel.

If my workouts were scheduled for the morning, I'd sometimes make a beeline to Einstein Brothers Bagels for an everything bagel with a smoked-salmon smear, a walnut cinnamon danish, and coffee. The bagel place is so close to David's studio, sometimes I was still out of breath from my workout when I ordered. It feels pretty stupid ordering a danish while dripping with sweat. It's like asking to be doused in kerosene while you're already engulfed in flames.

For a long time now, the shame of eating fattening food never once stopped me from doing so.

Shame.

Shame about my weight has been part of my life for a long time. For nearly a decade I've barely been able to fit into my clothes. I've actually pretended to have another person in the car while I ordered food at a drive-thru. I've asked for two place settings from room service just so the person on the other end didn't think all the food was for me. At this point in my life, shame has taken on a whole new meaning. My ability to tolerate shame, to compartmentalize it, to swallow it, increased right along with my belt size. It came with the territory of being heavy. Obese people have a lifetime of experience with shame. It's our specialty. Ordering a danish just after a full workout was, well—par for the course. A numbness came over me. I felt it, but I'd gotten used to it long ago. At least I pretended that I had.

The worst lie was the one I'd been telling myself about my commitment to eating healthy. I'd spent the past few months pretending I was actively focused on changing my eating habits. In fact, I was really just dancing around the subject. Playing racquetball and exercising with David on a regular basis was a big upgrade from what I had been doing for the last twenty years. But the project's success was predicated on my delving deeper into my relationship with food. That process started with me finally admitting that I'm not just someone who loves food. I'm also a food addict and compulsive eater.

It was time for me to see a nutritionist and get some help.

I had been referred to Janet Zalman, a well-known local nutritionist, back in December. I stared at her phone number for weeks. Finally, I stored her contact information on my to-do list—where good ideas go to die. I knew I should call her. I promised myself I'd call her. I promised Brooke I'd call. I just couldn't bring myself to face her. A good nutritionist represents the most realistic mirror out there. Up to now, I'd been too scared for that kind of high-definition honesty about my body. I was willing to make jokes about it, but not to do the hard work necessary to understand my relationship with food without yukking it up and pretending it was funny. It wasn't.

It's not that I'm afraid of other kinds of self-discovery and analysis. To the contrary. My wife's a therapist. I see a shrink. But shrinks don't have scales in their offices. No shrink's going to make you get on a scale every week. That's what I needed—the scale.

Finally, in the first week of February I reluctantly called Janet's office and set up our initial consultation. Knowing that an appointment with a nutritionist would likely mean an end to all my secret eating, I went out for one last meal before we were scheduled to meet.

I'd scheduled the appointment with Janet for an hour after my workout with David. David's studio and Janet's office are a few miles apart. I had just enough time for lunch between sessions. A new Asian place called the Satay House had recently opened just up the road from Janet's office. I'd been meaning to try it, as I have a standing policy of eating at every Asian restaurant within ten miles of my home.

The place was empty, as it was well past lunch time. I ordered Vietnamese spring rolls and General Tso's chicken. The waitress uncomfortably pointed out that the General Tso's chicken lunch special already came with a spring roll. She asked if I was sure I wanted an extra appetizer in addition to the combo appetizer. Shame moment no. 5,897. Yes, I was sure. I muttered something about bringing home leftovers for my kids. Food lie no. 9,784.

Arriving at Janet's office for the first time, I still had the taste of lunch in my mouth. I felt like an alcoholic who got drunk on the way to rehab. I was disgusted with myself. Enough was enough. I was ready to get help, at least until my bloated belly digested all this food. After that, once the hunger returned—all bets were off.

I knocked on Janet's door. Perhaps because I was running out of room in the latest pair of fat pants, I was ready. I wanted help. I needed someone who could see through my games and little white food lies.

Janet's assistant, Carol, sat me down in the office and handed me a pound of fake fat. It looked like a big melted orange candle. I was told to hold it until Janet came in. There I sat, waiting for help, tossing a pound of pretend fat from hand to hand. It was a low, low moment. Time would tell if it was rock bottom, as I tend to collect rock-bottom moments like some people collect Beanie Babies.

Enter Janet Zalman. Janet is a registered dietitian. She's also the spitting image of Sally Jessy Raphael— glasses and all. She was dressed to kill. I guess it makes sense in her line of work. She's in her fifties, fit, styled, confident, and she was quite sure that I'd hit my goal if I listened to her and stopped eating like I was trying to prove a point. At least one of us believed in me.

"Why are you here?" she asked.

"I'm trying to lose fifty pounds in a year."

"By when."

"Next August."

"How much have you lost so far?"

"About fifteen pounds."

"So, you've got thirty-five to go?"

"Yup. And I've got till August."

"So, roughly six months . . . call it twenty-four weeks."

She did the math in her head. Thirty-five pounds . . . twenty-four weeks. "You've got to lose a pound and a half a week. It's doable, if you're absolutely serious about it and stay with it."

"It's my job. I'm serious."

If I was serious, I figured I might as well tell her about what happened back in August.

"This summer, I gained almost seven pounds in one month."

"*Seven?*"

"Eight . . . but who's counting?"

"Okay. That's *a lot* of weight to put on in such a small amount of time. It's extremely unhealthy for your system to do that."

"Nine."

"Nine what?"

"I gained nine pounds in a month."

"Not eight?"

"No ma'am."

"First it was seven, then eight. Now we're up to nine. Are we sticking with nine?"

"Yes, definitely nine pounds . . . I gained *ten* pounds."

"I feel like we're negotiating."

"Sold! Ten pounds, and that's my final offer."

She looked at me like the lunatic that I am. She realized what had crawled into her office. I was the Bob to her Dr. Marvin. Crazy had arrived at her door.

"Did you actually think you could do all of this without a coach, without help?"

"I figured I'd give it a try."

"How'd that work out for you?"

"Not so well."

"What are you planning on doing differently now?"

"I'm going to listen to you."

"Do you promise? I'm not easy to please."

"I'm married. I'm used to that."

We spent the next hour talking about my history with food. Janet was pretty sure that I'm both a compulsive eater and (at times) a binge eater. I should have kept my mouth shut about gaining all that weight back in August. Regardless, she was right. I'm far more of a compulsive eater than a binge eater—but I truly am both. Knowing that, defining that, saying that out loud, was a big step.

Hi, my name is Ed, and I'm a total fucking mess.

Hi, Ed!

Compulsive overeating is characterized by uncontrollable eating followed by feelings of guilt and shame. It is different from bulimia in that it does not involve any purging. While it inevitably results in weight gain, it is also not to be confused with obesity. Not everyone who is overweight has an eating disorder.[1]

Men and women living with binge eating disorders suffer a combination of symptoms similar to those of compulsive overeaters and bulimics. The sufferer periodically

---

1. Brown University Health Education Website, http://www.brown .edu/Student_Services/Health_Services/Health_Education/nutrition_ &_eatingconcerns/obesity.php

goes on big binges, consuming an unusually large quantity of food in a short period of time (less than two hours), uncontrollably eating until they are uncomfortably full. The weight of each individual is usually characterized as above average or overweight, and sufferers tend to have a more difficult time losing weight and maintaining average healthy weights.

Binge eaters use binges as a way to hide from their emotions, to fill a void they feel inside, and to cope with daily stresses and problems in their lives. Binging can be used as a way to keep people away, to subconsciously maintain an overweight appearance to cater to society's sad stigma against the overweight. The person may feel he is fundamentally undeserving of love, and if he can assign being fat as the reason for his feelings of stigmatization, he can avoid addressing those deeper feelings. It's like a preemptive strike against potential emotional threats. As with bulimia, binging can also be used as self-punishment for doing "bad" things, or for feeling bad about yourself.[2] If you defeat yourself first, no one can do it to you.

As you can see, this was no picnic. When Janet laid all that heavy stuff at my feet, she really took it out of me. I came in still believing I was a foodie with a wee bit of a weight problem. I walked out with a double-headed eating disorder. Intense stuff to hear about yourself—especially when you know it's true.

---

2. www.something-fishy.org, a website for people with eating disorders

I had a burning question for Janet, one on which the entire project might hinge. Can a compulsive eater also be a foodie? Was it possible to have, or at least develop, a healthier relationship with food and still get to have the good stuff every now and then? It's not like I could give it up cold turkey. Was this woman telling me that I could no longer love food, that I had to walk away from an old friend, one who'd been with me through thick and thin?

Her response allowed me to put my hari kari sword back in its sheath. Janet told me a secret, *the* secret, to healthy living—and it turns out I was the poster child for making it happen.

The people who can most successfully lose weight and maintain a healthy lifestyle are foodies. When it comes to healthy eating, people who know how to cook and make ingredients taste good have a distinct advantage over those who can't.

I know how to cook. I know how to make things taste good. Tell me more.

And she did. She'd knocked me off my feet by labeling me a compulsive eater. Then, she picked me right back up again by showing me that I had a real way out of this mess. I could . . . ahem, have my cake and eat it too. Once I described my cooking methods and what I typically prepared, Janet was thrilled. She wanted me to keep on cooking—morning, noon, and night.

One of the promises I made before I left that first appointment was not to eat out at all for that first week. I was to do a smart shopping trip at the market and then cook every single meal I ate all week. If I was willing to do that, she promised me results.

I promised.

I walked out of there with my mind bouncing around like a Super Ball. In one hour, I learned a hell of a lot about myself, about my relationship with food, and what I needed to do to fix what had been broken for a long, long time. There was plenty of bad news. But there was also real hope. For the first time in years, I felt optimistic about my eating. Someone out there actually thought I could do this. She gave me vitamins. She gave me a meal plan. She gave me a strategy. She gave me a much-needed kick in the pants. She charged me $600 for eight visits.

I hadn't had a strategy for my health in . . . well, ever really. Damn it, now I had a plan. I was shocked at how good that felt. I walked out of there like Rerun after the Doobie Brothers let him off the hook for bootlegging their concert. I was high as a kite, and scared to death. I wasn't so much depressed as overwhelmed. Some highlights:

- I'm a compulsive eater.
- I'm a binge eater.
- I'm in trouble.
- There is hope.
- Janet can help.
- I'm a cook. I can help myself.
- I can still be a foodie, just a different kind of foodie.

- I can lose 4–5 pounds a month.

- I can lose one pound a week.

- Janet's kinda mean.

After I gave him the details of my first meeting with Janet, David said he actually wasn't the least bit surprised that it had taken me that long to start seeing a nutritionist. He believed that once I started seeing a nutritionist, I knew that I'd have to stop eating and start doing the hard emotional and psychological work associated with losing weight. Playing racquetball and exercising with a trainer had their own benefits, but, more importantly, neither endangered my ongoing relationship with food. I can play all the racquetball I want, see David all week long, do all the sit-ups, push-ups, and crunches that are required of me, and still protect the one area of my life with which I wasn't yet willing to separate—my eating.

Now that Janet was on the scene, especially with her take-no-shit attitude, I could no longer eat what I wanted and get away with it. She'd bust me if I did. I needed a food coach in the same way I needed David when it came to exercising. Someone had to make me care more than I did when I was on my own. Someone had to force me to eat right. Plus, the weekly weigh-in that Janet mandated mattered to me. I wanted that scale to go down each and every Monday. It was nice to know I still had an ego under all that fat. I found myself making different decisions, better decisions, because I knew I had to to get on that scale.

Chapter 5

It snowed last year, too. I made a snowman and my brother knocked it down and I knocked my brother down and then we had tea.

—*Dylan Thomas*

The only thing worse than waking up at the crack of dawn in the dead of winter is waking up at the crack of dawn in the dead of winter to go work out with your sadistic trainer. It was late February and I was in the middle of a very intense few weeks of workouts with David. Not only were we seeing a lot of each other, but I was pretty sure we were playing a game of chicken right at that point. Every day for the previous week or so, when we finished our workout, he told me that the only opening he had in his schedule for the next day was at some god-awful time like 7 AM or 9 PM. He was testing me. He had other times free. He was just looking to see how committed I was to working out.

I was committed. What choice did I have?

For the last few weeks, I'd been showing up and working hard when I was in his studio. But lately, I'd been complaining that I was getting tired. I also made the mistake of telling him that I went a wee bit off the diet one week. While he never overtly judged me, I knew he was disappointed. Thus, David had little patience for my cranky moods. I'm convinced that his way of punishing me, as passive-aggressive as it may be, was to make me come to his studio at inhumane hours. We were both digging in for a long fight, because I wasn't about to say uncle and he wasn't about to let me get away with eating poorly and complaining about exercising—not on his watch. Meanwhile, I was privately beginning to crack. There was no way in hell I'd let him see it, but I was having a hard time keeping it together working out this much.

I felt like he could tell when I was eating poorly. It's as if he could see it in my eyes. He's a bit of a witch in that way. Maybe it wasn't that dramatic? Maybe I just kept showing up with mayonnaise on my T-shirt? Regardless, the guy was in my head so much that I was actually getting afraid to eat. He was intimidating me and that was driving me crazy. Every time I thought about food, I saw David shaking his big head in disappointment. He was completely taking the fun out of eating. In a way, he was forcing me to stay on my diet—in spite of myself.

At that point, I much preferred going to the club and playing racquetball to working out over at David's. Racquetball hadn't changed since I was a kid, save for all kinds of improvements to the racquets. However, I was twenty years older and sixty pounds heavier. For me, it was a whole new game.

Nearly every Saturday and Sunday morning from the time I was eight until well into high school—if we weren't

fishing at the beach—my brother, Phil, and I played racquetball. Weekend racquetball was not up for discussion.
Like it or not, we were playing—Dad's orders. If we were
sick—we'd better be at death's door. If not, we were expected in the car by 7:15 AM.

Unless you have a brother, it's hard to accurately describe the level of competition that exists between two
male siblings—especially those close in age. Phil and I are
only a year apart—Irish twins. Add a healthy dose of pu-
berty and hormones and you've got yourself one heated
Saturday morning racquetball game. Phil and I were very
close. We still are. But our racquetball sessions were often
intense, at times too intense for anyone's good. Some of
the ugliest fights we ever had took place in that cement
shoe box.

There were days when we acted like animals just because a few people stopped to watch us play as they finished their coffee. Once we saw a few heads watching—an
already heated match became a roaring boil. Sometimes
tempers got out of hand. Sometimes feelings got hurt.
Sometimes things got downright violent.

The escalation of tensions on the court was ritualized
and not without its poetry. We had ways of sending each
other signals—warning shots of impending doom. Because a well-hit racquetball can travel up to 150 miles per
hour, that little blue ball was quite a statement maker.

One way to get your brother's blood flowing was to
return his serve by making the ball scream just past his
ear—scaring the crap out of him in the process. A rubber
ball zooming past your head that fast makes an unmis-

takable hissing sound—think angry hornet defending nest. Not only do you hear it, you actually feel it. When you're done making sure you're not dead, your fear quickly turns to anger . . . at Phil.

Once one of us picked a fight, the other would answer in kind. Soon enough, the score became somewhat irrelevant. The game turned into a wild session of chicken. We'd never actually accuse each other of trying to do what we both knew we were doing. That would be . . . uncivilized. We just had to just sit there and take it—until we couldn't take it anymore.

Inevitably, the warning shots would escalate into madness. We'd eventually just start hitting each other as hard as we could with the ball. Still lightly veiled as "mistakes," each return was a powerful forehand into the other's arm, leg, or kidneys. The inner thigh and calf were particularly prized targets. Any place with exposed skin was a home run.

Words cannot describe the pain.

Getting hit by a ball going that fast feels electric, like you've just stuck your wet hand in a socket. When it happens, you think that the pain will never go away. Once that first wave of pain subsides, it occurs to you that your *brother* did this on purpose. This pain, this mind-numbing pain, is all *his* fault. You try your best to swallow the pain, because there's no goddamn way you want him to see your eyes well up with tears. Plus, there's incentive to getting over it and starting to play once again. Revenge. Revenge is a dish best served into your brother's nuts.

Some days, I'd try to make a smiley face of bruises on

Phil's back. Phil would simply aim for the same spot on my body over and over again—making one mega bruise so ugly I'd wince upon seeing it after a night of sleep.

There were times when Phil would simply lose his mind on the court. Audience or not, he'd tire of my antics and, instead of hitting me "by mistake" during a point, he'd just start aiming for me *after* the point had ended. That's known as assault.

I'd start running around like a madman, screaming for our dad—or anybody—to help me. The coffee-sipping club members who were watching us would stand there with their jaws on the ground or, not quite sure what they were witnessing, inconspicuously back out of view. Sometimes, Phil would actually seal off the door so I had no exit. Invariably, I'd end up tucked into some corner of the court, rolled up like a potato bug—crying—while Phil whaled the ball at me. He wouldn't stop until I made a run for the exit or he simply tired of hitting me and left the court himself. Then, I'd just lie there in a puddle of pain and embarrassment—plotting my revenge.

On the days when Crazy Phil would make an appearance, the ride home with Dad was stony and silent. The tension between his sons was obvious. Dad's typical response was to get madder at the two of us than either Phil or I were at each other. Dad would get so angry, Phil and I would quickly reunite—bonded once again in our collective fear of Dad's temper. It was a bizarre type of emotional hot potato. I'm sad, Phil's mad, Dad's happy. Next thing you know, Dad's mad and Phil and I are kissing his ass so he snaps out of it before we get home and he takes it out on the whole family. The delicate dance of the Ugel household.

How do you snap Dad out of a bad mood after morning racquetball? Feed him.

At least once a weekend, Dad, Phil, and I would head to dim sum after playing racquetball. (And some people simply drink Gatorade.) Back then, dim sum wasn't nearly as *en vogue* with Westerners as it is today. Back in the '80s, the three of us were often the only non-Asian people in the entire restaurant—always a good sign in an Asian restaurant.

We were regulars. Before we'd even put our napkins in our laps, the women pushing the carts would descend on us and start piling plates on our table. They knew what we liked. It was there, in the aftermath of our racquetball matches, that I first ate so many of the things I love today: steamed shark fin, pork or shrimp dumplings; fried taro root with shrimp; football-shaped pork and mushroom dumplings, fried "half-moon" dumplings with pork and shrimp, roast pig with sweet soy sauce, roast duck, baby clams with black bean sauce, turnip cake.

Flash forward twenty years and because of the Fatty Project, racquetball finally reentered my life. The first time I played racquetball this past year was with my brother-in-law, Ari. Ari and I are very different. I'm a talker; Ari is quiet and reserved. I can eat until someone pries me from the table; Ari eats in a very temperate way. I spent the fifteen years after college not exercising; Ari is an exercise freak. I'm heavy; Ari is rail thin. We genuinely like each other. But we are almost polar opposites.

For me, Ari is the road not taken. For Ari—my life's a morality play.

Several times a week, Ari plays squash at our health club. I didn't know or care how good he was at squash. As a racquetballer, I always looked down on squash players as snobby pricks who walked around the club with their little badminton racquets feeling quite superior to us racquetball guys. I still feel the same way. Squash is a plague.

One day early in the project, Ari invited me to play with him at the club. I figured I'd mop up the floor with him. It wasn't even his sport.

"But you're a *squash* player," I said. "I should hang you from a nail by your jock strap."

"I can play racquetball. I'll borrow someone's racquet."

"You don't even have a racquet? You have no idea who you're fucking with, slim."

"I'm sure I don't, but let's get your fat ass on the court and find out."

"You can't handle the truth."

"The truth is that you haven't done anything but smoke weed and eat bagels in twenty years."

"Your point being . . . ?"

"My point being that I'm going to beat you so badly that you won't want to come home and tell your wife about it."

These were more words strung together in one sentence than I'd heard Ari say in three months. I was intrigued.

I was also confident. I had a decade of skills under my belt. Granted that decade had dust on it, but I knew what I was doing. Plus, this guy plays squash. Their ball doesn't even bounce. They have these cute little racquets. Some squash players even wear collared shirts when they play—no doubt with the collar up, the preppy bastards. Yes, I was a bit out of shape. But I just couldn't see myself losing to Ari.

Know thyself.

Ari gave me the beating of a lifetime. He didn't simply win. He embarrassed me. We played four games. These were the actual scores: 15–0, 15–1, 15–0, 15–2. If this even makes sense, the games weren't as close as the scores show. To his credit, he was all class after we played. He didn't rub my nose in it. Frankly, I think he was too worried that I might keel over and drop dead. I was wheezing for air out there. I couldn't catch my breath.

While the beating stung, it also got my racquetball juices flowing again. I wanted to play more and more—just with someone other than Ari.

Enter my friend Skipper. Skip is as disturbed as I am. No matter what the adventure or misadventure I've been on over the last twenty years, odds are that Skipper was there with me.

It turns out we're unbelievably well matched on the racquetball court. While I started out with more skills, Skipper's no pushover. He's in much better shape than me. Moreover, you've never seen anyone hustle like he does. He's "that guy" out there—diving and sprinting after every ball. He never gives up on a point, whereas I've made a career out of giving up. In an average game he'll leave his feet and dive at least twice, which is twice more than I ever dive. I might skin my knee.

The best thing about playing with Skip is witnessing the rare occasion when he loses his temper. He's never once yelled at me. Even when I deserve to be yelled at, he'll just swallow it . . . and swallow it—until BOOM. Skipper will lay into himself in a way that would make a truck driver blush.

The problem with Skipper's cursing is that a racquetball court has the echoes and acoustics of an opera house. Whatever you say goes bouncing off the walls and out into the world for all to enjoy. It's really bad when someone walks by just as Skipper calls himself a "fucking pussy" or "weak-ass bitch." Good times. Your first instinct is to hide, but there's just about no worse place to hide than in a glass-enclosed racquetball court. Lab rats have more privacy.

Skip's cursing gets really interesting when school's out. The health club runs a popular indoor tennis and squash camp during summer days. Every time we play, scores of kids ranging from age five to sixteen hang out and watch us. It's a veritable day care center in there. Included with all these kids are their parents, picking up or dropping off little Timmy for his squash lesson only to hear Skipper screaming, "MOTHERFUCKER!" at the top of his lungs. Ah, the expressions on the faces of Bethesda's most well-to-do mommies looking into our court. Priceless. You'd think we were monkeys throwing feces at the glass.

The project also allowed me to start playing with Phil

for the first time since we were kids. These days, he's a great sport on the court. I should add that he's never once cornered me and tried to wedge the ball between my butt cheeks like he did when we were growing up. That in and of itself makes him a better partner.

Like me, Phil hadn't picked up a racquet in decades. As it was for his little brother, suddenly sprinting all over a racquetball court for the first time in years was an absolute shock to his system. After a few minutes playing our first game, he was beet red; I thought we should stop playing. I got concerned. This is not the way you want your brother to die. Try explaining that to his wife—or our mother. With all his wheezing and sweating, I figured I was going to win every game in style—as long he didn't drop dead. Instead, he beat me senseless in the first game . . .

and the second . . .

and the third . . .

and the fourth.

The highlight of the match was when I mistakenly whacked Phil with my racquet as hard as I could on the left side of his belly. But other than making that perfect waffle pattern on his side, I had a humiliating day—one of many since we started playing again.

Within a month of my first game with Ari, I was playing with either Phil or Skip four to five times a week. It was odd how evenly matched we all are. But it's a streaky game. There are weeks where no one can beat me, followed by weeks where I can't seem to win a game to save my life. Much as with dieting, my racquetball prowess comes and goes. Still, regardless of the outcome, I love playing. I get great pleasure—perhaps an inordinate amount—from winning on the racquetball court. Losing makes me question my own existence.

Beyond all the hyperbole about the psychology of winning, I was just so damn happy to be exercising again. It may not be profound. It may not be a lofty observation. But it's true. For my entire life, even the rare times when I've been in shape, the gym was where other people went—not me. Even during high school, when I was still a good athlete, I never went to the gym unless a coach made me. I got by on whatever talent I had, not hard work in the weight room. I never had the discipline to work out. I never had the willpower to take care of myself like that—even back then. So to find myself willingly going to the gym nearly every day, was downright amazing.

I went from being completely intimidated by the club to a regular. I knew some of the staff, which showers had the best water pressure, which lockers smelled better than the rest, the shortcut up the back stairs to the old racquetball courts, where that weird guy with the old school Chuck Taylors hung out in the mornings stinking up the entire row of lockers. I wasn't just a member at the club, I belonged there.

At a certain point it finally dawned on me what all the fuss was about. The gym was actually . . . fun. More importantly, my time there was my own. It wasn't about the kids or my wife or anyone else. Ironically, the place I used to avoid like a roomful of cops had become a respite of sorts. I worked in my basement, so I was rarely out in the world doing my own thing. The gym filled that void.

I went. I worked out. I played some racquetball. I would have a steam, maybe sit in the sauna for a bit. Was I there because of the Fatty Project? Yes. But I never expected to feel so at home.

You want to fit in at the gym? Get sweaty. Walking around with a shirt full of sweat is perfect camouflage for whatever insecurities you brought in with you. You could be dragging around Jimmy Hoffa's head, but as long as you're sweating, no one gives you a second glance. Everyone's doing their own thing and honestly couldn't care less about who you are or how you look. It took me forever to figure that out. I think a lot of people—myself included—believe that they need to be in shape to feel comfortable at the gym. Once you go a time or two, you see how silly that is, much like the insanity of cleaning up before the housekeeper comes. The gym needn't be saved for those who are in shape.

I started off with small goals at the gym. Early on, I wanted to lose enough weight so that I could wrap one of the club's unnecessarily small towels around my belly. A modest ambition, but it seemed more apropos than aiming to bench-press my own weight or jog on a treadmill for an hour.

When I first started going to the gym, I was too embarrassed to even think of showering. There was no way I was going to stand there being all fat in front of a bunch of strangers. I just didn't want to deal with the whole scene—the community showers, the steam room full of sweaty strangers. Luckily, my aversion to bathing after a workout didn't last long. The first time I played racquetball with Skipper and told him I wasn't going to shower afterward, he looked at me like I'd just admitted to falling in love with a poodle. It wasn't until Skip shamed me into it that I finally took a shower at the gym.

Soon enough, I cherished my steam and shower time. I loved sitting in the steam room, sweating out toxins and perhaps even yesterday's ill-advised scoop of ice cream. As my body sweated, I fantasized about how much weight I was losing with each passing minute. If I could have, I'd have stayed in the steam all day.

The steam room and showers at the club are nothing fancy. No matter the time of day, everything pretty much smells like feet. Still, they did the trick. And I'd come a long way. I could walk naked around the locker room without hyperventilating. It wasn't exactly cruising down South Beach in a Speedo (my secret goal), but I was in public with nothing to cover me except a tiny towel. Strange as it may seem, this was growth.

By the way, Sasha had at this point forgotten about that scary night when she thought the CPAP machine was attacking me. Now, at the ripe old age of four, she'd grown quite fond of mocking me every time she saw it. When she saw me wearing the mask, say in the mornings when she got up, she would call me "Dumbo." Her grammy taught her that—bless her heart. Most days, Sasha made sure I understood the reference by explaining that Dumbo is an elephant.

Yes, sweetie . . . Daddy gets the joke—just like yesterday.

Chapter 6

The obese is in a total delirium. For he is not only large, of a size opposed to normal morphology: he is larger than large. He no longer makes sense in some distinctive opposition, but in his excess, his redundancy.

—*Jean Baudrillard*

Another two months, another twelve pounds. It was March, and I was down about thirty pounds overall. It was obvious that I'd lost weight. I could see my face again. I was wearing pants that didn't have elastic waistbands. Brooke had stopped looking at me as if I were an exhibit at the state fair.

It was all coming together right then, at the end of a long winter. I was playing racquetball. I was working out with David three to four times a week. Some days, I'd even work out with David and head right to the health club for an hour of racquetball and a steam. That's like three hours of exercise. You can eat almost anything when you're working out that much. Believe me, some days I tried my best to prove the point.

I was finding real success eating smaller portions of food I love. It seemed like something I could stick with for the long term. I didn't feel deprived of anything then.

If I wanted it, I ate it—but just a bit of it. I'd much rather split an appetizer of prosciutto and mozzarella with someone than have my very own big salad. I can't do salads for too long without burning out. But these little portions of delicious, interesting food were keeping me out of trouble.

For the two months, I hadn't once gone too far off course. I'm convinced it's because I was allowing myself to have almost anything I wanted, in moderation. Did I miss eating a pile of Buffalo wings? No, because I was still eating Buffalo wings—but just a few. That twentieth wing tastes the same as the first one does. At that point, I was absolutely content with a few wings and some veggies. It's hard to feel denied when the food you desire is in your stomach. It was too hard to get *none* of what I wanted, but I found it pretty easy to settle for just a bit of it. Combine the controlled food portions with all the workouts, and I was looking at a manageable lifestyle. I was enjoying myself, and it was showing.

I liked my progress, especially given the time of year. I liked that I'd been working out in the dead of winter. And now, I was noticing some early buds coming on the trees. Soon enough, I could get back outside and walk the trail again. I actually missed the trail. I was used to missing different things, like Vegas. It was a nice change.

Winters have traditionally been my worst time of year for dieting and exercise. But David took weather off the table. He expected me at his house, rain or shine. It was interesting spending so much time with David. Our relationship was evolving. We were becoming friends. I'd never had a fifty-four-year-old-gay-hunky-trainer friend. It was cool. He's wild. He's weird. He's gentle. He's different. He's funny. He's nuts. I found myself confiding in him more than I did with anyone else in my life. It was strange, because I'd barely known him a few months before. Now we'd gossip like old yentas. If nothing else, time sure flew when we exercised together.

I actually looked forward to getting on the treadmill at David's. There were a few days that spring when I practically moved into his place, as my house was under siege by the unlikeliest of people. One day Emeril Lagasse's "team" pulled into my driveway. I thought they'd never leave.

Talk about poetic justice. I'd spent the last decade telling anyone who'd listen why I didn't like Emeril Lagasse. (I'm not a fan of the "bam" stuff.) Yet there they were, a camera crew for his new show, *Emeril Green*, camped out upstairs in my kitchen, filming Brooke and her sister, Mara, as they pretended to cook organic vegetables. The good news? Emeril himself was not in my house. But worry not: Brooke and Mara were going to shoot with him the next day at a local Whole Foods Market. Emeril and Brooke? What is this, Mad Libs? Brooke on a cooking show was like Mel Gibson headlining a panel about Jewish culture.

There's no doubt that Emeril is an excellent chef. I've had great meals at his restaurants. I've learned a thing or two from his cooking shows. I've just never gone for his folksy chatter with what always seemed to be the world's creepiest studio audiences. Everybody would always ooh and ahh every time Emeril cut a damn pepper. And I never understood why the hell they were clapping when he just added flour to some melted butter. He's making a roux, like he does on every episode. Why are you so happy? He'd say "garlic," and the place would erupt in applause like he'd just cured AIDS. Fortunately, his new show was being shot in a working Whole Foods Market. It was just Emeril and that day's guest. There was no audience for him to pander to. He couldn't really shout "BAM!" without looking like a moron.

So how then did Emeril's TV crew end up in my kitchen? Brooke and Mara applied to appear on Emeril's show under the bullshit premise that they wanted his help coming up with new, exciting, healthy food ideas to make for dinner every night. Along the way, someone on the Emeril team also came up with a fraudulent story line that both of our families receive a shipment of local organic produce delivered to our houses each week.

Apparently, Emeril was going to use Brooke and Mara's "delivered" produce as a launching pad for fun, accessible menus for our two families. Lucky us. Meanwhile, they shot a scene at my front door where one of the guys in the TV crew pretended to be our nonexistent produce deliveryman. They filled a box with store-bought vegetables and filmed the poor schnook walking up our steps, ringing our doorbell, and delivering the "farm fresh" produce to my wife—who just happened to be waiting by the door—in full makeup—looking beautiful and ready to cook. (Yes, I know—it sounds like a porno.)

Brooke and Mara are the two most honest, decent

women I know, but they thought nothing of pretending to have organic vegetables delivered to our house . . . for the good of a faux story line. In reality, the only food that gets delivered to our house is pizza or Chinese. And Brooke cooks dinner for our family about as often as I get on the roof and clean the gutters. I do the cooking round these here parts. Thus, all things being equal, I didn't like the fake premise of what they were shooting. I didn't understand why the whole show had to be based on lies. This wasn't an episode of *24*. Couldn't the truth be good enough for a cooking show? Here's a premise for you. My wife can't cook. Can you teach her? *Bam!*

You'll be shocked to learn that I was a total joy killer about this whole thing. Like the antisocial nut job that I am, I pouted in the basement all day long, giving the busy TV crew my famous "Don't mess with me" look I'd perfected over the years. So, yes, I was playing the part of moody husband in the basement. As a result of my attitude, Brooke was furious with me, making it that much more likely that she'd end up lopping off her finger as she pretended to know what she was doing with a knife in her hand. I was 80 percent sure this whole thing would end up in the emergency room with Brooke bleeding all over some organic brussels sprouts.

A few months later, the Emeril episode aired. Everyone came over to our place to watch it. We took a few pictures of the TiVo guide listing the show with Brooke and Mara's names right there for everyone to see. We all gathered around the TV as if the Beatles were playing Sullivan. I had to admit, the show was great. The girls looked lovely.

Brooke even had a few moments of witty banter with Emeril.

Emeril was exceedingly kind to both Brooke and Mara. He was a real mensch. It was a nice thing. It gave Brooke and Mara a lot of pleasure, which made me happy. All night long after we watched the show, I felt like a putz about how I acted during the taping. No one went out of their way to disagree.

The highlight of the show? At one point, they were all outside grilling a bunch of food in the Whole Foods parking lot. Emeril was doing most of the work while Brooke and Mara followed along asking questions and assisting in one way or another. This was the best exchange between Emeril and Brooke.

"My husband says that you should leave most of your food alone on the grill and really only flip it once, in order to get a nice sear on the meat. Is he correct?"

"He's absolutely right. He knows what he's talking about."

Gotta love Emeril. *Bam.*

When my attorney, Ben Feldman, found out I was trying to lose weight, he had two pieces of advice: do a cleanse and get a colonic. Leave it to a lawyer. That little tip cost me $346. Still, Ben knows what he's talking about. He's safely navigated me through shark-infested legal waters. If the guy tells me to wash out my colon, I'm washing out my colon. I've had attorneys tell me worse.

Ben had recently lost a bunch of weight on his own, a fact he couldn't help but remind me of three or four

times during our phone conversation. As I sat there, paying Ben by the hour, I was particularly interested in hearing him detail—over and over again—how much happier
he was now that he was thin. I was glad to know that his
self-esteem was peaking while I was having a hard time
sleeping through the night without dying. Thanks for the
ego boost. So glad I called. I got off the phone feeling like
André the Giant.

Ben also told me that the latest health craze in Manhattan was BluePrintCleanse. BluePrintCleanse is a rela-
tively young company that caters to our better selves
when we're desperate for help after we've continuously
plied our bodies with gin and red meat for months and
years on end. The company is run from a warehouse in
Long Island. Zoe Sakoutis, the founder and co-owner,
started the business out of her apartment just a few years
ago. Today they've become the premier juice cleanse program in the city. They even ship nationwide. Their corporate mission is to make people run the risk of accidentally
crapping themselves all over the nation. They're well on
their way.

BluePrintCleanse was born when Zoe Sakoutis caught
a cold. Back in 2000, a hard-core cold knocked her out of
commission for an entire week. Desperate for some sort of
relief, she turned to a "raw-foodist" friend for guidance.
That friend recommended that Zoe try a seven-day juice
cleanse. Though the cleanse absolutely helped her get
back on her feet, she also found the entire process over-
powering and unnecessarily hard on her system. Zoe, like
99.9 percent of us, was unprepared for the impact that a

powerful juice cleanse had on her body. However, she had an idea. What if you developed a cleanse that was tailored to an individual's specific dietary and health needs? Could you market a more user-friendly cleanse? Was there juice in all this juice?

Zoe quickly realized that if others were going to find success with a cleansing product, "it had to be more than just a single, unforgiving process for everyone regardless of individual habits. If people were going to reap the benefits of cleansing, they had to want to do it, and want to do it regularly. It needed to be easier for them, particularly when they were just starting out, and needed to be customized to their level of nutritional awareness and dietary history."[3]

Zoe brought in a public relations specialist and avid foodie, Erica Huss Jones, as her partner. Erica has described herself as "a former model and certified yoga instructor with a fondness for martinis and a passionate relationship with cheese."[4] My kind of health freak. Together they developed the different juice combinations used in their cleanses and launched the brand in early 2001. By the time they heard from me, they were well on their way to becoming the most popular juice cleanse company in Manhattan . . . one poop at a time.

A few minutes of research on their website tells you that the program works best if you have one or two

---

3. www.blueprintcleanse.com
4. ibid.

colonics before and after their three- to seven-day cleanse. It's a cleanse. Do the math. These folks are serious.

I'd never done a cleanse and, shocking as it may seem, I'd never had the pleasure of a colonic. Frankly, it was a toss-up as to which one interested me less. On the one hand, there's the absolute indignity of having your insides hosed down like a frat house basement. On the other, you're drinking nothing but whacked-out fruit and vegetable juices for a week, doing God knows what to your body, and likely wishing you were dead. In the real world, you'd sooner catch me at a Glenn Beck book signing than trying either one of these healthy adventures. Not my bag.

I decided to be open-minded. I'd seen *Survivorman.* I was no Les Stroud, but I could surely go a week without eating real food. And, as far as my reaction to a tube squirting five gallons of warm water into my colon—time would tell. Let's see old Les try *that* in the middle of the Amazon rain forest.

I decided to do both—the cleanse and the accompanying colonics—after I called my dad (a dermatologist) and confirmed that I wouldn't get a disease or some awful ass rash. You better believe that once my dad said I could do it, my wife got on board. I found five free days in my schedule, took Sasha to school, got a haircut, picked up the dry-cleaning, and learned Japanese . . . I was gonna do it . . . soon.

Just to be safe, before you do anything involving your anus, I highly recommend a cursory Google search to educate yourself. It just makes sense in this day and age. When you Google "colonic" it's important to have your search filter turned on. (Learn from my mistakes.) And no matter how tempting it may be, *do not* add the word "sex" to the search—even if you're just trying to amuse yourself. Furthermore, if you do search for "colonic sex" and haphazardly click on a link for www .asseaters.com, I strongly recommend you don't give them your credit card. Under no circumstances is that a wise decision. If you happen to have given them your credit card, I urge you in the strongest way possible to save your username and password, as the motherfuckers won't let you cancel your monthly subscription without it.

A colonic, also known as colonic irrigation or colon hydrotherapy, is an alternative medicine treatment that involves flushing the colon with either purified water, herb-infused water, or water with coffee grounds. If you use coffee grounds, may I suggest a Kona blend? Kona is a dark, flavorful, full-bodied coffee with a mellow character and pleasant aftertaste. Doesn't your colon deserve the very best? Also, contrary to what, in hindsight, some would consider an obvious point—don't add cream and sugar to the coffee grounds. It doesn't end up making any difference.

The alternative medicine community claims that colonics keep the immune system strong and remove long-standing waste, which they say is harmful for both digestive and overall health. After thirty-six years or so, fecal matter tucked into the nooks and crannies of your colon starts to actually get in the way of your body's ability to get nutrients out of your food. The alt-meds think that this can lead to various health problems associated with lack of vitamins, minerals, amino acids, and other things your body needs. A colonic scrubs out your colon, making your digestive system squeaky clean and ready to suss out whatever nutrients are in a plateful of Ring Dings.[5]

After a few weeks of threatening myself with false deadlines, I finally called the folks at BluePrintCleanse and told them I was ready for my first shipment. Never one to go it alone, I convinced David, my loyal trainer, to do the cleanse with me. He hardly needed a cleanse. He's in great shape. He decided to do it for two reasons. First, he was trying to be supportive. He wanted me to succeed more than I did. He had skin in the game now, right along with me. He figured that if he did the cleanse too, I'd be far less likely to fail . . . or quit. Also, he wanted to try the Blue-PrintCleanse so he'd know whether or not to recommend it to his other clients, many of whom were on the lookout for something to jump-start their health regimens.

Finally, he's loony tunes, cuckoo, out of his mind. What on earth was he thinking?

David was just so damn excited about the cleanse, I had to refrain from hitting him in the groin. He couldn't wait to get started. Whereas I felt like Ed Norton counting down the last few moments before he went to jail in *25th Hour*. I was dreading the whole thing, and David was acting as if we were about to depart on a cruise.

---

5. www.wisegeek.com

In an e-mail, Erica was adamant about the need to taper down my heavy food intake in the week prior to the cleanse. When I made a joke about not listening, her response was, "Don't say I didn't warn you."

Even though it's exactly the opposite of what the BPC directions were, I'd been eating like a horse. They said to taper off your intake of booze, heavy meats (steaks, chops, blood sausage) as well as cheeses. Ideally, you'd have a light diet consisting of fish, fruit, salads, and veggies for a week or so prior to the cleanse. This way, your body will feel less impact on day one. There won't be so much junk in your digestive tract for your body to deal with while it's being inundated with kale juice and other demonic concoctions. I'd decided to go in another direction. While David was doing as directed and tapering down, I was eating whatever I wanted, basically choosing pleasure now over the likely pain and discomfort my body would feel once I got started. If this cleanse couldn't flush out some pepperoni pizza and a few martinis—it was their fault, not mine.

In the BluePrintCleanse world, there isn't just one cleanse; they've got an entire line. How long you cleanse for and what level of cleanse depends on your current health regimen. You choose the duration and intensity level. They handle the rest. There are three-, five-, and seven-day cleanses. There are also three levels of intensity: Renovation, Foundation, and Excavation. On their website, there's a brief description of which product is right for each customer, as follows:

The Renovating Type

"I know what whole foods are, and I've seen people buying them. I would too, but I'm too busy to be choosy—my vegetable intake comes in the form of ketchup (tomatoes) and French fries (potatoes). Salad is found in EVERY cheeseburger I eat—it's that greenish color in the middle of the burger. Fruit? Easy, it's the garnish on my cocktail (usually an orange). I have cut back on red meat, and know I should only buy organic, free-range, hand-massaged meats and vegetables raised by people who smell like patchouli oil, but where do they even sell that stuff?"

The Foundation Type

"I don't know what I am! I'm not a vegetarian because I eat fish (but not the kind with mercury). I'm definitely NOT, nor will I ever be, a vegan—(I love a good cheese plate . . . and sometimes a salumi plate). I try to eat a big salad every day and limit those 'bad starches.' When I do have dessert, I order some sort of fruit-based dessert, as opposed to that awesome flourless chocolate cake . . . that sometimes I do order . . . but only because it's flourless . . . and a special occasion. But that's not even a big deal, cause I'll just work it off at the gym the next day."

The Excavation Type

"I am extremely conscious of everything I put into my body. I exercise, I don't make drinking a habit, and I eat organic. Am I a vegan? A raw foodist? I'm not into labels, so when people ask me that question, I simply reply, 'I eat what I want, when I want it.' I don't consider choosing my food wisely 'missing out.' My only rule is: if it doesn't make me feel healthy and zaps my energy, I don't eat it. I'm not trying to live forever, I just want to make sure that while I am alive I feel as good as I possibly can!"[6]

This may come as a shock, but I'm not an Excavation type. I don't even know any Excavation types. Even the description listed on their website rubbed me the wrong way. I'd happily pay extra for the opportunity to punch an Excavation type in the stomach. One day soon, maybe I'll work my way up to becoming a Foundation type. They seem like okay folks. Alas, that day is off in the distance. I can see it but I'd be fooling myself to think that I qualify for that label today.

I'm apparently a Renovator—and that's just because they have no other options. The description isn't exactly on the nose. I get what they're trying to say in their too-cute-by-half marketing text. The Renovator level is sup-

---

6. www.blueprintcleanse.com

posed to appeal to a guy like me. I just don't think they've ever come into contact with someone quite so demented when it comes to food.

They actually made the wise decision *not* to appeal directly to my particular demographic on their website. I think they should consider having one more secret category reserved for writers who are grossly unprepared to do anything like this. (Think the secret menu at In-N-Out Burger.) Some of us were there to get good material, or were on a dare from our wives. Did they have a level that fit *our* needs, perhaps one sponsored by Hershey's chocolate or Stolichnaya vodka? Was there a Pre-Renovator level? Maybe a Happy Meal cleanse—perhaps something that comes with a windup toy or temporary tattoo?

Grudgingly, I signed David and myself up for a five-day Renovation cleanse.

We put a lot of thought into timing—trying to figure out during which five days we'd miss food the least. I was due to go fishing with my friends Skip and Ben down in Delaware (an annual trip that involves nothing but food, booze, and a bit of fishing—if we can pry ourselves away from the TV). Typically, we come home from this spring fishing trip feeling like Mickey Rourke in the '90s. I would be drinking and eating everything in sight for three days, after which I swore to myself that I'd never drink alcohol or eat fatty foods ever again. Timing the cleanse to coincide with my return from the fishing trip might just work.

On the basis of this scientific approach, David and I set the start date for April 21. My body might do quite well with a week of healthy cleansing after the trip, but the notion that I'd "ease into it" was a joke. Three days at the beach for the food/fishing trip with Skip and Ben meant no time put aside for healthy living. Consequently, the cleanse was going to hit my system like a tsunami.

The one concession I made was that I'd detoxify as best I could the day before. Sadly, the day before meant on the three-hour drive back from the shore. That ride back normally consists of coffees, pastries, burgers, chocolates, caramel corn, and whatever else was leftover from the weekend. This time however, I'd have to quit all my debauchery cold turkey and start fasting right there at the beach. It would be a long, sad drive home.

On my last evening at the beach, my BlackBerry delivered this e-mail from the happy marketing folks up at BluePrintCleanse:

> *Hello Cleanser!*
>
> *By now you've probably made it through your first juice and asked yourself at least once why you decided to embark on this somewhat strange and green journey. The answer lies ahead—your body will thank you at the end of it all!*
>
> *As you have already been advised, this cleanse is what you make it. The closer you stick to it, the better the results will be, but hey, you get props for even getting this far, so we want your experience to be as enjoyable as possible.*
>
> *INSTRUCTIONS: When you begin on your first day, start off with some water or water with lemon.*

Hot is best, but room temperature is just fine too. This is to wake up your system and get things moving. From there, drink your juices in their numbered order as often as you need to. Because we're not all operating on the same schedule, a good rule of thumb, as far as when to drink (the juice), is to wait at least one hour between drinks and to finish the last beverage at least two hours before you sleep. Consuming anything before or close to bedtime does not allow your insides proper rest.

Throughout the day, keep flushing your system— drink water, green tea (regular or decaf) and herb tea, as much as you like. Just keep it coming! If you notice you are having . . . trouble . . . (which is totally natural, as you're not taking in any fiber while on green juices), some flaxseed oil added to the juices or an herbal laxative is an excellent way to keep things moving. (See our website for suggested brands under "how" and "hydrate & eliminate.") Make sure that you drink your last juice no later than 8 PM, so the body can finish digesting and get to work cleaning those organs for the night!

Other tips for the full benefit of detoxification:

- *Try getting a massage to help those toxins move on through.*

- *Exfoliate! Scrub away dead cells and reveal your new healthy skin.*

- *Colonic hydrotherapy—The Full Monty! If you're up for it, there is no better time to do this than after you finish your cleanse.*

***Cheater–Cheater–eating–during–your–
cleanse–eater:*** *While we recommend you abstain
from food during your cleanse, we realize you just
can't resist; so if you're going to do it, at least be safe.
The main thing to avoid is extra acid like vinegar or
Tabasco, or salt—these will interrupt your digestion
and make you feel . . . funny. And not funny ha-ha.*

- *a few celery stalks*
- *a quarter of an avocado*
- *a couple slices of cucumber*
- *dilute any drink with water*
- *warm vegetable broth (low sodium)*
- *a half cup of black coffee (no sugar)*
- *drink half of the cashew nut milk in the* AM
- *add a pinch of Celtic sea salt to any drink for
energy*

*Please feel free to send questions along and we'll
try to help you as best we can.*
All the best!

The e-mail burned my eyes. They just couldn't be
more excited for me to get started. Aw, shucks. I felt like
I was headed to God camp. Admittedly, they were nailing
their customer service. I just didn't share their enthusiasm.

Sitting at the beach, in our rented town house, with a steak-n-cheese sub in my hand, my cocktail glass just refilled—I wasn't looking to hear from my wife, much less the people at BluePrintCleanse.

Their e-mail pep talk fell on deaf ears. They had me as of Monday morning. This was Saturday night. This was still my time, my sandwich, my eighth cocktail, my ice cream waiting patiently for me in the freezer. Monday morning was impending doom. I didn't need a reminder e-mail. I deleted it and finished my sandwich. Still, the reality of the e-mail sat on my chest like a weight the rest of the night. They were waiting for me: the juices, the emasculating colonics. Once we finished off all the cheeses, the pâtés, the salumis—payback was imminent. No matter how much I drank, how much I ate, how late I stayed up that night . . . they were coming for me. Monday morning was racing my way, there was nothing I could do about it—so, I ate.

Day One: Monday, April 21

I had two colonics scheduled in the next eight days. Two. That's twice as many as the poor bastard who's just getting *one* colonic. Still, there was a part of me, a big part of me, that was thrilled to get started. How long could I pretend that all this eating and obesity was a riot? I was dying. I could feel it. I could feel my body telling me that it couldn't keep up. I was the world's ugliest man.

Mentally—the toll of all that weight was immense.

Yes, I'd lost a good amount of weight, but depression still found me. I was ashamed of myself. I was tired of all the food. At this point, there was little pleasure in eating. It was now just something I was programmed to do. There were still days when I didn't leave the house unless I had to. If I remained heavy, soon enough my weight will start affecting the girls. Soon, they'll be old enough to notice . . . and care. They weren't getting the best me. How could they be? I was not at my best because I didn't feel like myself. I was so wrapped up in thinking about my weight problems, I had to be missing something with the girls— with Brooke? I dreaded the cleanse but at the same time I couldn't wait to start.

The five-day supply of juices came in two separate shipments. Because the juices are not pasteurized, they are highly perishable, with a shelf life of only a few days. So the company staggers your five-day supply. I was planning on working out with David all morning, so we had both shipments delivered to his house.

As promised, two boxes arrived just before ten o'clock. I'd never been so disappointed to see the FedEx guy in my entire life. Opening my box was depressing. Imagine the worst Christmas gift ever. Inside was a three-day supply of juices. Each day consisted of six numbered bottles. I was looking at my squeezed and pressed breakfast, lunch, and dinner for the next few days. Even worse, another FedEx was scheduled to arrive in two days with the final twelve bottles for each of us. Oy. Thirty bottles in all . . . thirty bottles to go.

It's hard to describe the color of the first juice. It wasn't so much inviting as it was intimidating. Don't think apple, orange, pineapple, or cranberry—not even close. Imagine what it would look like if you threw a gray cat in a food processor and added tons of seaweed. That's juice number 1. Juice number 1's actual ingredients are romaine, celery, cucumber, kale, parsley, green apple, spinach, and lemon. I guess the lemon is like a garnish on the world's worst cocktail. Apparently, juice number 1 is so vital to the process that the identical concoction reappears as juice number 3. So, I had that going for me later that day—seconds.

David and I both put on a brave face, vigorously shook our bottles, toasted to our health, and took meager little sips of juice. My first reaction? It wasn't too bad. It was manageable, better than I thought. David's first reaction? He loved it. Perfect. He was acting like he'd just popped open a Fresca.

"You like it?" I asked.

"You know, I DO!" he all but screamed.

"You're not just saying that?"

"No. You can really taste the veggies."

"Of course you can taste the veggies. What'd you expect it to taste like, a milkshake?"

"I'm just trying to be positive."

"Well, don't. It's not helping."

"Well, it's helping *me*."

"Well . . . you're supposed to be helping me. I think it tastes like bad, cold soup."

"You know—it does. It really does. Thanks for putting that in my head."

"My pleasure. Welcome to hell."

David gulped down the rest of his bottle. "BREAKFAST!" he shouted as he visibly tried to shake off the flavors oozing down his throat like a kid waving off the taste of medicine. "I LOVE IT!" he said, this time more for himself than me.

"Yeah, right." I mumbled. "Sell that shit to someone who's buying." Following his lead, I tried to finish mine in a few big gulps. The taste got worse. "You realize we're gonna start cramping soon, don't you?" I burped.

"This will either kill us or—"

"—give us the runs?"

"Or give us the runs. Right on the nose, my friend."

"I'm kind of hoping it just kills us."

Truth be told, it wasn't that bad. It was fine. Better than fine, maybe. It's a cleanse. What did I expect it to taste like, a Yoo-Hoo? It doesn't. I think what struck me was knowing that this was the first bottle of many. Like it or not, there were twenty-nine more to go.

We finished our workout with the beguiling taste of kale on our breath. Toward the end of every session, David always made me do crunches and push-ups. Back in August, when I first met him, I struggled to do five crunches. All I could manage was three crunches and four push-ups. There was clearly no place to go but up. And, despite my on-and-off discipline thus far when it came to food, I was somewhat astounded by the changes in my strength and endurance. That day—fueled by juice number 1—I did one hundred crunches and seventy push-ups (not in a row, mind you—but all within about ten minutes). I have to be honest—I was thrilled to do that many crunches and push-ups. It might not impress someone who works out on a regular basis, but it made me feel . . . not so worthless.

I waited until around one o'clock to drink the second juice. Juice number 2 was a major upgrade from 1. The ingredients for number 2 are pineapple, apple, and mint. The only thing this one needed was about three fingers of rum and some crushed ice. It would make an excellent beach cocktail—probably not what they were aiming for up at BluePrintCleanse headquarters. If I had to find one thing to complain about, it would be that number 2 is very acidic. For all I know, that's why I was drinking it. Acidity notwithstanding, the juice was delicious. Maybe I liked it because it was lunchtime and I was hungry? Maybe it was because number 2 was such a massive upgrade from number 1? Regardless, it was mint, pineapple, and apple—I could imagine myself ordering it off a menu somewhere. It was no spicy chicken leg from Popeye's or heaping pile of Vietnamese grilled pork, but it tasted good and put me that much closer to getting through day one. At that point, I just wanted to get through day one. Plus, I had much bigger problems at the moment. My first colonic was in an hour. Looking down the barrel of that gun, the taste of the juice paled in comparison.

I know the objective of a colonic is to get rid of everything in your colon. I just hoped my colon could hold on until I was ready. As I drove to the appointment, the first two juices started to make my stomach . . . less stable. Things were getting rather bubbly down there. Not good. By the time I got there, I was a gassy, nervous mess.

It didn't help that I was sitting in some random, beat-up homeopathic medical office that just happened to be next door to a bar I'd been frequenting since high school. The clinic was in a storefront in my old stomping ground. I used to date a girl who lived a few blocks away. One of my favorite Asian joints was directly across the street. I could see our favorite table from my perch on the edge of my seat there in Poopyville. My current favorite dive bar was also across the street. I'd done a lot of living on that stretch of land. I'd eaten well. I'd drunk too much. I'd fought with my wife. I'd seen dozens of films. I took my kid here for a slice of pizza after her first ride on the Metro. And now, I was going to search and destroy old fecal matter out of my colon—all within a stone's throw from the bars and restaurants of my youth. There's no place like home.

When I'd called the previous week to set up my appointment, I ended up prepaying for a "three-pack colonic special." (No one's easier to sell than a salesman.) As per the BluePrintCleanse recommendation, I knew I was going to get two colonics. Buying three of them up front basically meant that I got the last one for free. A no-brainer, right? At worst, I could always give away the last one to someone else. Brooke's birthday was coming up in May. I never know what to get her. Problem solved.

Sitting there in the waiting room, it occurred to me that I was about to have an extremely personal, intimate encounter with a total stranger. There was poop involved, for God's sake. And this stranger could be anyone. It could be my old algebra teacher, or a Penthouse Pet. It could be that guy who sold me a used Acura back in 1998. Did I care? Should I care? I cared. Someone was about to navigate me through the delicate world of colon hydrotherapy. Someone was about to see my sphincter. *I'd* never even seen my sphincter. I cared a lot. What if it was a man? What if it *wasn't* a man? Did I want a woman? What if she was pretty? What if it was my ex-girlfriend? What if I got aroused? What if it was a man and I got aroused? Am I gay? Oh my God—I'm gay. What if I'm gay? What if I liked the colonic? What if I became addicted to them? Should I have prepaid for a six-pack instead of just three? Why didn't I just splurge and buy six? I'm such a fool. I wonder what the price break is if you buy a dozen? Can you imagine the look on their faces if I tried to buy a dozen colonics? They'd have me arrested.

To say the least, my mind was not right. I was all jacked up on bizarre fruit and vegetable juices. I hadn't had my coffee that morning (they said not to). I was on the precipice of a major bout of lemon-and-kale juice diarrhea. A vacuum cleaner was about to get shoved into my anus. Did I really need this? It was all I could do not to get up and leave. Who'd know any better if I did?

On the plus side, I was dying with curiosity about the whole thing. I'd heard stories. Now I was going to find out what all the fuss was about.

I was smart enough to weigh myself before I left the house. I weighed 229.2 pounds—a full thirty-four pounds

less than when I started. Whatever happened there that
day, no matter how terrible, or pleasurable—I wanted to
know what I weighed afterward. I could finally answer the
question of just how full of shit I really am. In an hour,
I'd have a quantifiable answer to that long-standing
query. It was worth all the drama just to know that. How
could I back away from such vital information? I owed it
to myself to know. If I were guessing, I'd say I was 2.3
pounds full of it.

I was daydreaming about random people giving me
a colonic when I heard them call my name. *See you soon,
Cher. Later, C-3PO.*

If I could have handpicked my colonic person, the
woman who greeted me in the lobby was as close as I could
hope for. Denise was an African American woman in
her late forties. She was covered head to toe in hospital
scrubs—including little disposable booties. (I guess disposable is the way to go in this line of work.) As she walked
toward me, her scrub-wrapped thighs made a funny swish-
ing noise like the school nurse who told Sloane that her
grandmother died in the beginning of *Ferris Bueller's Day
Off.* She reached out to shake my hand. A wave of calm
came over me. She was perfect.

"How you doin', darling?"

"Um . . ."

"Kinda at a loss for words?"

"Exactly."

"First time?"

"Exactly."

"Thinking about making a run for it?"

"Exactly."

"I bet you a dollar you'll love it."

"*Love it*?"

"Okay. I'm sure you're gonna *like* it."

"I don't know if I want you to be right or wrong . . ."

She introduced herself and navigated me toward a back room with a massage table inside. Adjacent to the room was a small bathroom. Although it had some unique modifications, it was nothing more than a tiny bathroom. This whole thing was going to take place in a bathroom? *You've got to be kidding me.* In hindsight, I'm not sure what I was expecting, but this wasn't what I had in mind.

"I need you to get undressed and put on this robe," Denise said. The robe was made out of paper and cut to fit an average-size Pygmy. Not that this was an ideal place to feel bashful, but come on. Nothing to cover up my privates?

"How undressed?"

"Take off everything but your socks."

"I can keep my socks on?"

"They'll be up in the air, out of the way."

"Up in the *what*? Where will the rest of me be?"

"Right there."

She pointed to the oddly modified toilet. There was a foamy chair-back attached to the front of the toilet. I had no idea what the hell was going on. Where were my feet going? How were they going to be up in the air? Where was the rest of me supposed to be? Was this really just a toilet with a recliner chair attached to the front? Where were all the fancy machines and spray guns?

Denise took a deep breath and gave me the standard introduction. You could tell she'd done this before, but I'm not sure she'd ever given this information to someone quite as bug-eyed as her current client. I was supposed to straddle the toilet and lean backward, with my ass hanging over the bowl. My socks could stay on, as they were going to be placed on the wall above the water reservoir (where the toilet's pump and flushing hardware reside). So I'd be sitting backward on the toilet, facing the wall, lying back at a 90 degree angle with my ass over the bowl and my feet on the wall. I wanted to call my dad and have him pick me up, like he did in the old days when I got scared at a sleepover.

It suddenly dawned on me why this place was so much cheaper than the others I found online. It was a dump. A clean and sanitary dump, but a dump nonetheless. I'd unexpectedly found myself in a Motel 6. I sort of imagined this whole adventure going down in a spa-type environment. I was hoping the place would look like the Four Seasons or at least a Hyatt. Not even close. This was a tiny, dilapidated half-bath in need of a paint job. There was even duct tape keeping the vent fan attached to the ceiling. I swear.

Second thoughts notwithstanding, I waited for Denise to leave the room and took off my clothes—except the socks. I put on the paper robe, which left my ass and penis exposed by several inches. I somehow backed myself onto the toilet-bench-chair, and did my best to center my ass over the bowl. The size of the bathroom made it needlessly difficult to get into the right position. I felt like a nervous, naked astronaut trying to get situated for a flight to Mars. Then, when I looked up from that unique viewpoint, I saw the water and the hose.

The water was stored on a rickety shelf above the toilet. It wasn't some special medical contraption. There was no dedicated pipe pumping in filtered water from a secure location. It was a five-gallon bucket, the same thing that we use to keep bait alive at the beach when we fish. The very same jug that held thirty pounds of pickles in cold-storage when I was a short-order cook back in Portland. The same jug in which Sherwin-Williams sells five gallons of paint to handymen. For all I know, the five-gallon jug of "filtered water" I was about to FedEx into my anus was once home to something far less sanitary—coleslaw perhaps?

Ever wonder how to shove a colonic tube into your butt?

Let's get one thing out of the way that I was relieved—and maybe a little disappointed—to hear. To my great surprise, the technician doesn't actually touch you "down there." You're basically flying solo the entire time. You've just got a friendly copilot nearby to tell you what to do and make sure you're okay. Remember that car with two steering wheels in driving school? Just imagine that Denise is the driving instructor but the wheel is actually a clear plastic tube you stick up your ass. Now drive.

Once I was in position, Denise poked her head into

the cockpit-size bathroom and handed me the business
end of the plastic tube that traveled up the wall and into
the bucket of water. She also handed me a tiny package
of Vaseline. I've never been so happy to see Vaseline.

"Can't we just talk a little first? I feel like we hardly
know each other."

"This is gonna take a while, sweetheart. We'll have
plenty of time to talk."

"Shouldn't I call your parents before this gets serious? It would be rude not to introduce myself, don't you
think?"

"My parents are dead."

"I'm sorry to hear that . . . It wasn't colonic related,
was it?"

"No."

"What if I have to pee while it's happening?"

"You won't have to urinate."

"How do you know?"

"You'll be too busy."

"Too busy to pee? Never. Ask around."

"Do you want to urinate right now, before we get
started?"

"No . . . I could use a cigarette."

"Tell me about it. I quit years ago."

"Me too, but it seems like a good time for one,
doesn't it?"

"Sure does."

"Are you at least going to tell me what to do?"

"The first thing you need to do is relax. It will make
this a lot easier. Put the Vaseline onto the tip of the tube—

lean back—take three deep breaths and let your sphincter relax."

Let my sphincter relax? If my sphincter were any less relaxed at that particular moment we'd have had to use the jaws of life to get in there. Maybe she could bust through with a chisel and hammer. Three deep breaths? Was there such a thing as anal Valium? That's what my sphincter needed—not air.

Before she ducked out and left me and my anus to ourselves, she showed me a little clip on the tube that I could pinch to increase, decrease, or stop the flow of water. When my colon was "full," I could pinch the clip and not waste the water. Yes, God forbid I waste the precious water—perish the thought.

"One last thing, Denise . . ." I whispered. "I don't understand how I'm supposed to get the water out of me once it's . . . up there. Do I pull out the tube?"

"Don't pull it out!" she said.

"Then how does the water get out?"

"It will flow right out. The tube won't be in the way."

Okay. Didn't know that little detail. Glad I asked.

"Would you like to try some spearmint?" she asked. Huh?

"Kind of an odd time for gum, no?"

"It's not gum. It's liquid that we add to the water."

"So, you're offering my colon a breath mint?"

"Sort of. It helps digestion. Try it, you'll like it."

My colon and I accepted the spearmint. Denise disappeared for a moment and returned with what looked like a shot of Listerine. She reached over me and dumped it in the water bucket hovering above. She told me that she'd be just outside in her office. If I needed anything I should just ring the doorbell conveniently located by my right ear.

And there I was, straddling a toilet—Vaseline in hand—anus in a terrible mood. It was time. I put every last drop of Vaseline on the end of the tube.

> B-R-E-A-T-H-E . . . . . . *I should have gone to law school.*
> B-R-E-A-T-H-E . . . . . . *No one's gonna want to read about this.*
> B-R-E-A-T-H-E . . . . . . *This is not going to win me the Pulitzer.*

Nothing. I tried again.

> *B—R—E—A—T—H—E* . . . . . .
> *B—R—E—A—T—H—E* . . . . . .
> *B—R—E—A—T—H—E* . . . . . .

I could feel my body relax. Air. Who knew? With that, I slid the tip of the tube into my rectum. Hello, Dolly.

The truth of the matter is, it was no big deal. The tube's about the size of a pen. It didn't hurt. It felt weird, but the whole day had been off-the-charts weird. It's not as if I wasn't expecting weird. I signed up for it—and here it was, about two inches inside my rectum. I took one last long, slow breath and pressed the clip, releasing the flow of water.

Boy, you sure feel *that* right away. It felt like someone was filling up a water balloon inside my stomach—fast. It feels like you've got to have a bowel movement—now. Your natural inclination is to try to hold it in—whatever "it" might be. I was holding on tight. I was confused. I wasn't exactly sure what was going to happen if I let go. I felt like I might fly away.

"Don't try to hold it in . . ." Denise called from the other room.

"I can't help it." My voice quivered. I was fighting off a tidal wave.

"Let it go."

"I don't think I can."

"Let it go."

Then I did. I just let everything go. It felt good, letting go.

Imagine a warm, not entirely unpleasant, forty-minute diarrhea. Everything that went in, came out—with friends. There's surely no question that you're cleaning out your system. All kinds of stuff's happening down there. It was fascinating.

I guess there are two kinds of folks in the world: those who look in the bowl and those who don't. I looked in the bowl. When it comes right down to it, I'm a look-in-the-bowl kind of guy. Maybe it's from a lifetime of listening to Howard Stern? I felt it was my obligation as an adult, as a father, to look in the bowl and make sure everything was okay.

Honestly, I was dying to look. When I did, everything was as you'd imagine . . . except for one thing. Floating there in the bowl was something that looked *exactly* like a champagne cork. I was mesmerized. Was it a cork? *My God! I think it's a cork. Maybe they just drop one in there to scare overly curious clients?*

I'm 99 percent sure it wasn't a cork.

Brooke had all kinds of theories when I told her. You should have heard the morons at my book club when I told them. I could have settled the matter by reaching in and touching it. I did not. I just couldn't. I thought I'd get in trouble if I got caught.

Clean up was a disaster. I've never wanted to get out of a place so fast in my entire life. I've hung around girls' apartments longer after a breakup than I stayed in that bathroom.

I was free to go, save for one last tip from Denise: You're likely to shit down your leg on your way home. *Have a nice day.*

Because my colon had just been waterboarded for forty minutes, you can imagine that there was still some water sloshing around in there. Denise warned me to give it five or ten minutes before I got dressed, just in case. No deal. I couldn't wait. I pulled the tube out, ripped off the paper nightgown, found my underwear, and delicately tiptoed out of there while trying not to get my socks wet.

I walked right to my car, hopped in, and crapped in my pants. Touché.

There was no hero's welcome when I got home. Instead, juice number 3 was waiting for me in the fridge. There would be no celebratory dinner to wash away the day's pains. Not tonight. If I hadn't been on the cleanse,

I'd have given myself the night off for good behavior and likely stopped for Chinese on the way home. Instead, I had four more juices to drink before I could put the day behind me. After all, nothing washes away the memory of a colonic like a cold cup of kale, cucumber, and parsley juice.

This was officially the worst day of the project thus far.

The second I got home, I weighed myself. I'd lost 4.2 pounds during the colonic. Four more colonics and I'd hit my goal weight. *How many times a week can you go?*

The four-pound dip on the scale took the edge off my foul mood. I called David to tell him about the colonic. It turned out he was not a happy camper. He was struggling with the cleanse—even more than me. I was shocked. I was worried. I was thrilled. We spent a few minutes talking each other off the same ledge. It felt good to know he was struggling too. It was going to be a long week, and misery loves company. I was glad he was doing it with me. We agreed to stay on course through the night and regroup in the morning.

Juice number 3 (the exact same concoction as number 1) was no picnic. My body was still in shock from the colonic. The strange veggie brew wasn't helping. At this point I just wanted some bread, something to stabilize my belly. Enough with the liquid. I followed the juice with a cup of chamomile tea, which was nice and soothing to my body.

I was definitely urinating a lot. Yet, I had no idea when I'd ever have another bowel movement. I felt like I just crapped enough to last me until Purim. What on earth was there left inside me at that point? And I'd be eating nothing but juice for the next five days. To say the least, I was confused about the impact the colonic would have on the rest of the week. How was I going to cleanse if I didn't have anything to poop out? Was I going to lose more than the four pounds I just "lost" during the colonic? Can you lose weight if you're not pooping every day?

Juice number 4 was quite good. It's basically spicy lemonade. The ingredients are water, lemon, cayenne, and agave. If it hadn't been the only thing I was eating for dinner I'd have been raving about it. If it were sitting next to a cheeseburger, I'd have been looking at a perfect summer beverage. But there was no cheeseburger here. It was just me and the lemonade.

It was dinnertime for the girls. Brooke was working late. I was going to make them dinner and put them to bed. I was baking some chicken nuggets in the toaster oven. They smelled divine. I'd never wanted a nugget more than I did right then. I was also making the munchkins some linguine with butter and Parmesan cheese, which they'd happily eat every day for the rest of their lives if they could. They'd already torn through the leftover green beans I'd steamed the night before. Now they were popping edamame (another favorite) while I finished up making the nuggies and pasta. They were oblivious to my bad mood—quite rightly. I was smelling the cheese and butter melt into the pasta and it was making my mouth water. I wanted to eat my children. Being in the kitchen really stank. I found myself mumbling mean things under my breath about Brooke not being home to help me, as if she'd left me there so she could go clubbing. She was seeing patients. I was just a grumpy, hungry jerk.

The girls and I played for an hour or so before I put Romy down for the night. Sasha gets to stay up a bit later than her little sister. Sasha and I spent about twenty minutes inside the purple tent her Grammy got her at the fair. Sasha informed me that we were on a camping trip to the moon. She started dressing me for the occasion. Apparently, the moon is best viewed with Daddy wearing a princess tiara and his socks on his hands. She reminded me that the moon was cold tonight so the socks would keep my hands warm. Good point.

"What about my feet? Won't they get cold on the moon?"

"No, silly. Your feet are inside the tent."

"Do they have a Popeye's on the moon?"

"Who?"

I sat wedged inside the tiny tent, with a tiara on my head, and drank juice number 5. Juice number 5 was so bad that I longed for the taste of juice number 1. Juice number 5's ingredients are carrots, apples, beets, ginger, and lemon. I loathe beets. While the rest of the ingredients in juice number 5 are fine, the beets dominated the mix. Consequently, I couldn't stand it. It was all I could do to drink it and keep it down. It wasn't the BluePrint-Cleanse's fault. I'm sure to a normal person, the juice would be just fine. To me it was a real challenge. But, seeing as Sasha and I were on the moon and all, I chugged it, shivered, took a deep breath, and gave her a bunch of tickles and pinches.

As always, spending time with Sasha made everything else fade away—even the beets. We decided to take a walk on the moon's surface so we could throw the red-stained bottle in the recycling bin.

"What kind of juice was that, Daddy?"

"It was moonshine."

"What's it taste like?"

"Beets."

"Do I like beets?"

"I think so. They're delicious and healthy for our bodies."

"Do they grow on the moon?"

"No. They grow in farms all over the country."

"Can I taste your moonshine?"

"Tomorrow."

The big payoff for drinking juices 1 through 5 all day was juice number 6. It was wonderful. Its ingredients are water, raw cashews, agave nectar, vanilla bean, and cinnamon. There was even some texture to this one. I could almost chew it, because the cashews, vanilla bean, and cinnamon all have a bite to them. Plus, it's the only juice that doesn't have an acidic base. It's almost creamy, like a melted vanilla milkshake. I drank it in bed at about 9 PM. It was so good, I made Brooke taste it.

Day Two: Tuesday, April 22

I got on the scale first thing in the morning. Not including the colonic, I'd lost another pound. Not exactly dramatic compared to yesterday, but I'd take it. I'd been drinking a lot of water, in addition to the juice, to help flush out my system. I'd never peed so much in my life. I felt like the cleanse was working. However, no bowel movement today. For some, that might be normal—but not me. I'm as regular as they come. I guess I shouldn't have been surprised given the events of the day before. Still, this was the first day in years that I'd gone without.

I went over to David's for a workout that morning. His weight loss was shocking. He'd lost ten pounds. TEN. I wouldn't believe it if I hadn't seen him get on the scale with my own eyes. He didn't even have a colonic and he lost twice as much as me. He was in great shape. I was Fatty. What gives? I don't even know where his ten pounds came from. He was putting on a brave face, but I knew the ten pounds had him scratching his head a bit. I sure was.

I got through the day without much trouble. Frankly, after I saw David and watched his weigh-in, I got super motivated. I didn't even think about cheating that day. The juices were definitely getting to me—except for the cashew milk. I loved that one. David was keeping me focused. He called in the evening to check in and swap notes. He really did seem to be struggling. He felt tired and weak. I asked him if that meant we could skip our workout the next day. He said no.

Day Three: Wednesday, April 23

David lost another five pounds. I hated him. He'd lost fifteen pounds in two days. I saw him on the scale, and I still didn't believe it. But mentally he was kind of cracking up.

He told me that he stood in front of his open refrigerator door Tuesday night, talking himself in and out of eating a few celery stalks and some avocado. He didn't. He should have. Who cares? He was only doing this to help me. The poor bastard was perfectly miserable. He was convinced that he was losing muscle mass in his arms. I thought he was crazy for not eating something. I appreciated his solidarity, but this wasn't his baby, it was mine. Plus, he was crushing me in the weight-loss category. I'd be just fine if he decided to have something to eat—maybe some pie?

Day Four: Thursday, April 24

Still no bowel movement. I just couldn't believe it. Other than that, I was fine. I was a little bitter, definitely feeling sorry for myself. I hadn't cheated, but I wasn't excited or feeling like it was a big adventure anymore. I was low on energy. I was sick of the juices. I hated them all—even the cashew milk.

I fed the girls dinner that night and raised my voice at Sasha for not finishing a blueberry yogurt. She'd eaten a great meal—full of vegetables—but I just couldn't let the yogurt thing go. I told her that some people would do anything to be able to have a blueberry yogurt. I added that some kids had parents who couldn't afford yogurt—really laying it on thick. Sasha started crying, which made Romy cry—which got Brooke going. I received a much deserved "how could you" look from Brooke which I happily returned with my patented "go fuck yourself" glare before storming out of the kitchen. I upset every woman in my family over a few spoonfuls of yogurt. Ta-da.

Daddy's hungry.

David called just after we put the girls to bed. He asked if I'd be disappointed in him if he ate a cup of soup and some avocado. I wasn't disappointed—only jealous. I was actually glad he was eating. He was clearly losing muscle mass. I could actually see it in his arms. He was down nearly eighteen pounds. Enough is enough. Some people just aren't as tough as me.

Day Five: Friday, April 25

As we wrapped up the cleanse, I decided to write Erica and Zoe an e-mail to get a handle on a few questions that had come up since we started. More than anything I was dying to know if David's extreme weight loss was normal or if we should rush him to the hospital . . . or Ripley's museum. Here's what they had to say:

1. What do you make of the rapid weight loss David experienced?

[The weight that is lost during the cleanse] is water weight—fluid pushes fluid and therefore flushes toxins, which should also help to answer the question of "how am I detoxing if I'm not having a

bowel movement[?]" The body eliminates in many ways beyond what comes immediately to mind. For example, through the skin, the lungs, urine, etc.

2. David (a fit, healthy, muscular, fifty-three-year-old, 235-pound man) experienced significant muscle loss. It was clearly visible in his arms. What do you make of the muscle loss?

This is about flushing your body of toxins and flooding your system with vitamins and nutrients and enzymes that one would normally never receive in such a short period of time. Because the calories are less than what you would normally [take in] in the form of cooked and processed foods, you typically lose weight and sometimes muscle. If you are a "big" guy and want to maintain or build muscle, you should add good proteins from whole and raw sources like avocado.

3. David and I are both "big guys." But, if I'm not mistaken, the portions of the cleanse juices that you prepare are the same, regardless of whether the client is male/female, big, small, etc. Am I correct? Would my ninety-nine-pound grandmother drink the same portion size as me? If so, I'm confused as to the logic. How can someone who weighs 260 pounds have the same nutritional needs as someone who weighs 110 pounds? Is that possibly why David experienced such intense weight loss?

This Cleanse is packed with vitamins and nutri-ents—it's not about calories, it's about nourish-ment and feeding your cells, not your belly. So we're not so concerned with deprivation here. The only time [calorie loss] is an issue is when one is breast-feeding, morbidly obese, or pregnant. That said, as mentioned above, supplementing the cleanse with raw extras like fruit and avocados is an acceptable way of adding more bulk to it without compro-mising the results.

4. In my case, as per your suggestion, I had a colonic the day I started my cleanse. Conse-quently, I had virtually no bowel movements the entire time I was cleansing. I was urinat-ing like never before. But I was confused as to how all the toxins etc. were leaving my body if I was not having a bowel movement. Your thoughts??

As a colonic really does work in tandem with a cleanse to completely clear your system from the in-side out, it is common to NOT have a bowel move-ment the few days following. But as above, you are still eliminating toxins via other outlets.

At the end of the cleanse, I'd lost nine pounds. David had lost eighteen. In the days immediately following the cleanse, David gained back fourteen of the eighteen pounds he'd lost. I gained back three of my nine pounds.

Was it worth it? Absolutely. More than the weight loss, the best part of the cleanse was the sense of accomplishment I got from completing it. It wasn't climbing Mount Everest, but I did it. I succeeded. It felt good to know that I could actually control myself and see something like this through from start to finish. I was pleasantly surprised with myself. While I'm patting myself on the back for not cheating, remember that Brooke was there watching me like a hawk. If left to my own devices, I hope things would have turned out the same way. I just don't know.

I'm a convert. There's surely something to all this cleansing talk you hear these days. I felt healthier. No matter how those little buggers got out, there were fewer toxins in me than there had been a week ago. That just has to be good for business.

For a fatty like me, a cleanse is also a heck of a jump start. If you actually go through a week of this, you're far less likely to simply throw it all away by eating poorly once you're done. You worked too hard to blow it—at least that's how I felt immediately afterward.

Chapter 7

There's nothing celery can do that either a cucumber or an onion can't do better.

—Donald "Skip" Holmes

I was lying in bed on an unusually quiet Sunday afternoon, half napping and half watching the end of the Nationals game on TV. Sasha and Romy had been on a playdate over at their cousin Elie's house. The girls came home while I was still asleep. I woke up to everybody laughing downstairs. Romy was wearing my CPAP mask. She'd managed to pull it off the machine and had actually figured out how to place it somewhat properly over her head. She was in the living room entertaining her mom and sister, swinging the long air tube from side to side, pronouncing that she was an "el-pants," while doing her best to sound like an elephant. The worst part was when I came downstairs, Brooke and Sasha quickly stopped laughing as if to spare my feelings. The word was out. Fatty was a bit sensitive these days.

My sensitivity notwithstanding, frankly, I was crushing the project at this point. April was the best exercise month I'd had by far. Out of the thirty days in the month, I trained or played racquetball on twenty-seven of them. I still feel like racquetball shouldn't count as exercise, as I'm practically addicted to playing these days. Regardless, it's a hell of a workout and just as healthy for me as anything else I do at the gym. That I'm not absolutely miserable while doing it—like I am on the treadmill or elliptical machine—is a brilliant stroke of luck on my part. I thanked my lucky stars that I'd found it again.

The lesson here's obvious: find something healthy that you love doing, and do it. Each day that went by, that point seemed more important than anything else I'd learned so far that year. That and don't eat Crisco.

Foodwise, April was a mixed bag. For the most part, I ate healthy: salad, grilled chicken breast, lots of fruit, grilled veggies with olive oil and spices, some roast pork loin. But I also had my fair share of food that was well off the plan—most notably, during the big happy-hour-Buffalo-wing kick.

Throughout the month of April, Skip, Phil, and I went straight to happy hour from the racquetball court. Yes, I know how that sounds. Yes, I know there's no excuse for me. No, I'm not recommending it to you. You should go directly home after a workout. There's a salad waiting for you, not to mention your kids.

Happy hour? Yes. Fatty likes happy hour. Half-price appetizers? Cold beverages? *Pardon the Interruption* on ESPN? A stool to sit on and break down the day's game? I'm in. We would play racquetball at around three. We would play for an hour, maybe an hour and a half. By the time we showered and got ourselves together, it was just about five. A fella gets mighty thirsty at the gym—parched even. Come five o'clock . . . happy hour just felt right.

We typically headed over to one of two places: the Dancing Crab, a crab house with a great dive bar, or this local high-end chain that reeks of corporate restaurant hell, but has fantastic Buffalo wings—if you know how to order them.

If you simply order the wings without any special instructions, you end up with a plate of soggy, mediocre wings—very disappointing. However, if you order the wings "double-dipped," the cook deep-fries the wings, coats them in hot sauce, and then deep-fries them a second time. The double-dipped wings are the best wings I've ever had. Frankly, no other wing even comes close. They are somewhat overdone, the skin perfectly crispy, the meat still tender. They are transcendent.

Needless to say, I've had a few wings in my day. Thus, when I say the double-dipped wings are the best wings around, I feel I'm somewhat qualified to speak of them in the superlative. However, what kills me is that they make you ask for the wings "double dipped" or they give you the crappy, regular-style wings. What keeps me up at night is the following: Who the hell would prefer the bad wings? Why not just make the excellent double-dipped wings the normal order? Why make it a secret menu option, available only to those in the know? *I'd* only known about the double-dipped option for a year, and I'd been eating their wings since 1902. This is the kind of worthless shit that I think about. I couldn't get them out of my head. Why not just double-dip everyone's wings?

Double-dipped or not, those happy hours with Phil and Skip were dangerous at best. Luckily, my drink of choice—vodka and soda—is about as low-cal as you can get at a bar. A vodka and soda cocktail has 82 calories, 0 calories from fat. In comparison, a Jack Daniels and Coke has 173 calories, 0 calories from fat. However, the Jack and Coke has 9.5 grams of carbs and 9.5 grams of sugar— the equivalent of three packets of sugar. A vodka and soda had no carbs and no sugar. It's not exactly "on" my diet, but I can handle the 82 calories . . . or the eventual 328 that I'll likely leave with before it's over.

Remarkably, all the weight training and cardio that David had me doing was making up for the happy hours. David taught me that I could actually increase my metabolism, thus burning more fuel, by building muscle mass. Muscles are metabolically alive tissue. All metabolically alive tissue requires calories or energy twenty-four hours per day, whereas fat requires no calories to maintain. The more muscle, the more energy your body needs to feed itself.

Your body will try to use food to make the necessary energy. In the absence of enough available energy, the body uses its fat reserves. Why do we diet? Put less food in the body, and the body burns the fat it already has for fuel. The more fat burned, the less fat on you. Consequently, the push-ups, crunches, and circuit weights that had been the bane of my existence for the past nine months were actually paying off. The nightmare-inducing weights were working.

My long quiescent metabolism was actually accelerating as my muscle mass increased. Not only am I looking more firm, but my newly built muscles—established 2008—were eating my stored fat cells. It was a labor of love making those fat cells. I imagine they were delicious.

How were my lungs now getting more oxygen into my body, thus allowing my muscles to grow? Cardiovascular exercise. The biggest result I saw from the cardio part of my workouts wasn't in my waistline, it was in my lungs. It turns out, all those hours on the elliptical machine and the treadmill were not just David's way of controlling me and making me feel like shit. Cardio is as important as he said. An emphasis on cardio in a workout routine has the following benefits:

- Cardio burns calories immediately.
- Cardio improves your capacity for oxygen uptake, which is critically important for building muscles.
- It is easier to maintain a habitual cardio exercise routine than many other forms of exercise.
- Cardio is fairly injury-free.

May was a rough month. My eighty-nine-year-old grandmother (Nana) fell and broke her hip. A broken hip is a bad deal for little old ladies. She'd fallen a few times over the course of the year. No matter what happened, we'd always say the same thing, "At least she didn't break her hip." Now she'd gone and broken her hip. It was heartbreaking.

The whole month, our family called and texted each other with short Twitterish updates about her hip-replacement surgery, her mood, if she'd eaten, if she was lucid, if she was in pain. She had the surgery just days after the fall. For a few days there in the beginning, they had her on so much pain medicine she made little sense, barely recognized the family, and was utterly paranoid. It was like visiting Gary Busey.

Dietwise, these days were murder. How do you stay on track when all you want is some sort of release after a day of watching a loved one suffer? Am I really supposed to go to the gym today? Am I supposed to choose a salad over the chicken tenders and pecan pie in the hospital cafeteria? Did I really just buy a banana from the coffee shop instead of a muffin? Me? How long can I keep this up? Who am I kidding?

On rough days like those, I don't want hugs or a shoulder to cry on. I want a rack of ribs. I want Popeye's fried chicken. I want braised pork belly. I want a meat lover's pizza. I want three dirty vodka martinis. I want an apple fritter. I want a Filet-O-Fish. I want pad thai. I want pastrami. I want pecan pie. I want mortadella. I want bacon wrapped in bacon. I want General Tso's chicken. I want to mainline MSG. I want to fill myself up. I want to be full. I want to be satisfied. I want to be overstuffed. I want to be a glutton. I want to eat and drink until I can't see anymore. I want.

I was trying to get used to the idea that I didn't deserve food just because I'd had a bad day. The food might soothe me, but it wasn't going to make Nana's pain go away, and it wasn't going to make me feel any better. Whatever I ate, Nana was still going to wake up with a bum hip. Food doesn't fix anything. It just makes your problems feel a little further away—like any other drug. Food addicts are like any other addict looking for a fix.

The facility where Nana was doing her hip rehabilitation is right near the old Tally-Ho restaurant where my mom used to take us when we were kids. I grew up on their milkshakes and cheeseburgers. Some of my earliest memories are housed in that place. Just seeing it after all those years brought back vivid memories. I could taste those bacon cheeseburgers. I could hear the old milkshake machine revving away, its blades scraping against the sides of the metal containers. I never liked that sound.

Once again, I was beset by the power of food in my memory.

One afternoon, I bought a coffee and a banana on my way to see Nana. I figured if I had food in my stomach and a hot coffee in my hand, the idea of a cheeseburger and a milkshake would seem less appealing. As I drove past the Tally-Ho, their neon sign flashed, "Open . . . Open . . . Open." The voice in my head reminded me of how good I'd been, how stressed I was, how cool that milkshake would be today.

For the moment, I pretended to love the grumbling in my stomach. I reminded myself that the grumbling meant I was losing weight. I told myself that showing some self-control was good for me. Anyway, the Tally-Ho was open late. They'd be there on my way home. I'd have yet another chance to pass or fail this never-ending test.

When I was growing up, food was like another member of my already crowded family. Sometimes I loved food, sometimes I was mad at it, and sometimes it made me sad. Sometimes it made out with the sixteen-year-old girl you were in love with at the Bryan Adams concert . . . no wait—that was my brother Phil. Just like any other family member, food had a role to play in our family dynamic, in our fights, our happiest times, and our worst times.

My obsession with food started at a young age. As a little boy, I loved to grocery shop with my mom. We couldn't pass a fruit stand without my curiosity being piqued. A new cereal hitting the shelves was breaking news in my world. Soft-baked cookies seemed to hit the marketplace just as I was old enough to ride my bike to the Safeway. It was kismet. I loved samples from the bakery and deli counter. *Maybe a gingerbread man took a nasty fall, rendering him unsellable? Is that grilled sausage I smell over in the meat department? Kraft has created a new pimento spread, you say? And I'm to spread it on this Ritz cracker? Well, isn't that wonderful. May I have one more to bring to my mother? Oh yes, aren't I a dear?*

Once I was seven or eight, my mom would let me order the cold cuts while she shopped in the rest of the store. I loved the meat slicers and the endless choices in the deli case. How did everything taste? Where did it come from? How did it stay fresh? What the hell was headcheese? After a while, I became a regular at the counter, a big shot, "Mr. U." I no longer needed to remind the deli guy to slice our meats and cheeses extra thin. It was understood.

Back then I thought the folks behind the counter got a kick out of a kid ordering food. In hindsight they likely found it annoying as hell. I'd play the part of the sweetest little boy in the world as they passed me slices of coppa, pastrami, Black Forest ham, cheddar, Jarlsberg, etc.

"How's the hard salami taste?"

"The same as it did the last three weeks you tried it."

"Oh. Good. Good to know."

I could work the better part of a snack out of deli samples, all while my siblings were back home riding bikes or sledding in the neighborhood. To each his own.

Being one of five kids meant plenty of birthdays throughout the year. Diet or not, birthdays meant a good meal and a homemade cake from Nana. She was an excellent baker. But I liked some of her cakes better than others. It would kill me to waste a perfectly good birthday on her ho-hum Harvey Wallbanger cake. I'd spend weeks negotiating with my siblings to request a certain kind of cake for their birthday. If they didn't have the common sense to avoid the Wallbanger, then I helped guide them in the right direction. It was for their own good.

I even loved the kitchen at school. I'd watch the staff fuss over huge pots of Charlie's Special (a chicken and vegetable stew) or sloppy joes. I watched the same lady peel carrots and potatoes like a metronome for six years. She was peaceful, not in a rush, but in a rhythm that changed little over the years.

When I wasn't critiquing my school's lunches or ranking the various cupcakes brought in by parents for their kids' birthdays, I was still thinking about food. What was for dinner tonight? I wonder if we'll go to the farmers' market after school? Why's a soft-shell crab soft? Is Nana making clam sauce this weekend? Is there actually corn in corned beef? Why's the top of Mom's chocolate pudding all leathery? Why won't Mom let us eat Wonder bread like everyone else?

While other kids were building rocket ships and airplanes out of Legos, I'd sit next to them snapping together the perfect BLT. Fortunately for me, my school nurtured my kind of "creativity." My teachers let me run with the food thing. I wasn't hurting anybody. They'd ask me what I was making, how it was cooked, if they could have a bite. The teachers at Sidwell were happy to let you make Play-Doh pasta. They'd even help you roll the meatballs. It was in this imaginary world that my interest in food began to grow. Between a school that supported my thinking about food as something worthy of my time, and a family that was passionate about food, I became interested in food in a way most kids never did.

In third grade, we spent a month learning about each student's heritage. It gave us a chance to tell the rest of the class about where our families came from, what that culture was like, what they ate, how and what they celebrated. Each day, a different student would make a presentation with a visiting family member who'd bring in a typical food from their country for everyone to taste. When my turn was approaching, I called my Pop-Pop.

My grandfather David Young was a successful local restaurateur. He and his brother, Paul, owned Paul Young's—a DC institution for decades. Paul Young's was an old-school, grand place, with a huge staircase leading to a formal dining room with chandeliers as big as Cadillacs hanging from the ceiling. The menu was classic Continental with hand-typed specials that changed every single day.

My grandfather and great-uncle had been in the restaurant business since they were kids in Philadelphia. During the Depression, they used to run a boarding house with their mother, feeding hungry dockworkers for a nickel a plate. Save for the years when they both served in World War II, they remained in the restaurant business until late in their lives.

In January of 1961, President Kennedy had his private pre-Inaugural party at Paul Young's. A few of the people in attendance that night were Frank Sinatra, Sidney Poitier, Tony Curtis, Ella Fitzgerald, Gene Kelly, Laurence Olivier, and Kim Novak. Kim Novak, one of the most beautiful women in the world, danced with President Kennedy as my then sixteen-year-old mother watched in wonder. While Novak was dancing with the president, the side seam of her dress split wide open. Nana took her into the back office and sewed her dress.

At one point that evening, Joe Kennedy, father of the president-elect, pulled my mom aside and introduced her to Frank Sinatra. Sinatra was beyond gracious. He took Mom's hand and talked to her for five minutes. At least that's the way the story's always been told. Sinatra holding Mom's hand in 1961? He was the biggest star on the planet. He made my mom feel like a princess. Gotta love Frank.

Toward the end of the evening, Joe Kennedy pulled Mom aside yet again. "Anyone else you'd like to meet?" he said.

Shyly, Mom replied, "I'd love to meet your son."

"Which one, my dear?" asked Kennedy, without missing a beat.

When Pop-Pop brought food to my third grade class, he went all out. Most parents brought in a little something from the homeland for the kids to taste. The Swiss brought chocolate. The Italians brought in some pasta. The Chinese kid's family had almond cookies. The French kid's mom made crepes.

Pop-Pop showed up just before lunch to discuss my Russian heritage. (I've got a Russian, Italian, and Greek family.) I figured he, like everyone else's family member, would talk for a few minutes and pass out something Russian—vodka perhaps? Not Pop-Pop.

Pop-Pop wheeled in a ton of food on a cart he must have borrowed from the kitchen. He served a bunch of third graders stuffed cabbage, borscht, blinis, and pierogis. I remember a handful of teachers from other classrooms started popping in for takeout. It was legendary. Food gets stapled to our memories like nothing else.

Regardless of what they were, Pop-Pop wanted us to pursue our interests. I told him I was interested in collecting coins, and suddenly I had a coin-collecting starter kit. My brother wanted to collect stamps. Same thing. As I grew older and my interest in cooking developed, my grandfather took it upon himself to help me along. Just weeks after my eleventh birthday, I told him I'd like to take a cooking class. Instead of looking into a class for kids, he called in a favor.

Jacques Blanc owned two popular French restaurants in Washington, DC, Chez Grand'Mere and Sea Catch. He was a real French chef—right down to his thick accent and obligatory chef's toque. In the early '80s, he opened the Jacques Blanc Academie, teaching local foodies the art of classic French cuisine. It was a place for serious food lovers—catering to the city's well-to-do cooks with a desire to upgrade their skills with a master chef.

One Tuesday afternoon, Pop-Pop picked me up from school and took me to my grandparents' apartment. We had fried salami sandwiches on rye bread with brown mustard and sauerkraut. He wouldn't dare fry salami if Nana were around—not healthy. But it was just us. He was safe. We ate and talked. After the sandwich, he slid me a Goldenberg's Peanut Chew which he always seemed to have hidden in his pocket. Then we were off to my first cooking class.

When we arrived in Spring Valley, a tony Northwest DC neighborhood, Pop-Pop turned down a small alley between Wagshal's Deli and the A&P market. Chewing on a mouthful of sunflower seeds, a habit he confined to his car and nowhere else, he leaned over and opened the passenger door.

"This is your stop. He's waiting for you inside."

"Who's waiting? We're in an alley."

"Walk right up those stairs. Chef Jacques Blanc. He's a great cook, and he's a friend. Call him 'Chef' when you first meet him."

"I'm not so—"

"Not so what, Edward? You want to learn to cook, right?" He said with a sliver of sunflower shell hanging off his lip. "Go learn."

"But we're in an alley. Can't I learn to cook somewhere with more . . . people?"

"There's plenty of people upstairs."

"Alley people?"

"Hey smart mouth, do one thing for me."

"Okay."

"Introduce yourself to everyone. And look them in the eye. Always look—"

"—Always look them in the eye. I know, Pop."

"I'll be back here at ten."

"Ten? Do my parents know that?"

"OUT!"

"But I've got a whole *Happy Days, Three's Company* thing going on Tuesday nights."

"OUT!"

"Love you, Poppers," I said, jumping out of his car.

"Look everyone in the eye and shake their hands."

"I will," I said, as the car drove away.

It was interesting that he didn't walk me inside. He always walked me in before. The poor guy never used to let me go to the bathroom alone. Maybe he thought I was becoming a man. That made one of us. Maybe he wanted me to have the confidence to walk in by myself? I surely wouldn't have minded his company just then. I was in an alley.

Walking up those stairs for the first time, I had no idea

just how much my life was going to change. Behind that door was a new world full of interesting people—people who loved food, who wanted to talk about food, who wanted to cook all day and eat all night. They were my foodie peers, except for one small detail—they were all adults. I was eleven.

These were real grown-ups with nice clothes and jewelry and jobs and kids and grandkids and mortgages and driver's licenses. I didn't have any of that stuff. My greatest possession to date was a tiny crop of newly arriving underarm hair. I had no car, no money, and no clue what I was supposed to do. I briefly considered showing everyone my armpits. I thought better of it and, instead, did as Pop-Pop told me to do. I walked in and started introducing myself to everyone—individually—looking them in the eye as I said hello.

Although the class always had a few people coming and going, the core group was there for the entire time I was. From the time I was eleven until I was sixteen, Tuesday nights were all about food, cooking, catching up with friends, and eating.

The three-hour class was broken into two sections: cooking a full meal from scratch and then eating it at a leisurely pace over many bottles of wine. I was far too young to drink, but the wine sure did flow. By the time dinner rolled around, you'd never seen such a cheerful bunch of people in your life. In hindsight, that might explain why they all liked me. They were looped.

Eventually, everyone came to know each other quite well. They all took great pleasure in taking care of me. I guess I was sort of the class mascot, which wasn't the worst gig in town. Still, once they realized that I took myself seriously as a cook, they did too.

After a few months, I made some incredible friends, none more so than Jacques himself. Already in his late fifties, Jacques was still every bit a father figure to me. He doted on me as if I were his own.

As much as I learned in the classes themselves, my real education came in the hours before class. Pop-Pop would drop me off directly from school, hours before the rest of the class would arrive. Jacques and I would then go shopping at the market together.

Shopping for food with Jacques was fascinating. A walk through the A&P with him was like walking through a museum with an artist. Everything was interesting. I learned the art of shopping—whether at the A&P or Dean & Deluca. There were lessons to be learned all over the market. Every Tuesday for nearly five years, I studied at the feet of a master.

We were an odd pair. He, a renowned French chef, and me, an eleven-year-old with nothing to do but watch, help, listen, and learn. He used the entire market as a classroom—my classroom. We took our time, walking the aisles, talking food. It would take us fifteen minutes just to pick out the best green beans or to find perfectly ripe peaches that we'd later use for dessert. He taught me how a piece of fruit should look when ripe, how it should feel in your hand, how to know a ripe piece of fruit simply by smelling it.

He taught me to be flexible in a market—how to let

the best-looking and freshest food decide what you were making that night, no matter how many folks you were cooking for. In the kitchen, nothing should be set in stone. Find the absolute freshest ingredients and make a meal around the product itself, not the other way around. If you went in thinking that you were going to make sea bass but the halibut looked better—make halibut.

Jacques taught me not to worry in the kitchen. I learned that in the end, you can make anything taste good as long as you take care of your ingredients. Your family, your guests will appreciate just having someone cook them a meal.

I'd watch the way Jacques talked to the butchers and the fishmongers, forging alliances with them so they'd keep something special for him when it came in. We'd spend hours in the meat department poking and pressing roasts and chops. He taught me the value of fat on a piece of meat—its marbled lines indicative of its quality and flavor. He'd reach right over the glass and pick up a whole red snapper, smelling it, looking at its lungs, pressing its eyes and passing it to me to do the same.

Whether I'm cooking for a party, myself, or shopping for the family—knowing how to get the best out of the market has helped me immensely over the years. Being able to shop well is one of the keys to losing weight in a way that a foodie can enjoy and maintain. Demanding the best-quality products and not settling for mediocre food is the first and most important step to being a successful cook and a healthy eater. It's a common shopping philosophy in Europe, but one that few Americans live by.

Once we finished our shopping, I'd help Jacques prep in the kitchen before the rest of the class arrived. What a thing it was to be his assistant at such a young age. Of course, you can imagine who peeled all the onions. As any good apprentice would, I did everything with passion. Along the way, he made sure to teach me a trick or short-cut wherever possible. Yes, I peeled dozens of yellow onions, but I also learned how to mince them during my private lesson. I happily peeled and sliced and minced and stacked and got his *mise en place* ready. It was a pleasure.

"Peel those onions."

"Yes, Chef!"

"Blanch the haricots verts."

"Yes, Chef!"

"Quarter these chickens."

"Yes, Chef!"

"Rob that bank."

"Yes, Chef!"

"Stab that man."

"Yes, Chef."

Once that evening's class began, I was deeply invested in the meal, because I had actually contributed to the process. I felt like I was in on a secret. *Wait till they see what he's gonna do with those artichokes!*

Jacques taught me to love the simplicity of great ingredients. How a scrambled egg can become something transformative—something perfect. How a ripe strawberry is as wonderful as anything you might cook yourself. He taught me knife skills. He taught me how to be creative in the kitchen, how not to care if you screw something up.

As he'd always say in his thick French accent, *"You can always order pee-zzahh, no?"* That lesson helped a lot over the years. Who cares if you try something and it fails? Who cares if you burn dinner? Who cares if you forget to defrost the steaks? Who cares if your timing is off and your entrée is ready before the first course? Who cares? It was great advice.

Jacques taught me to love everything about cooking—even something as mundane as peeling potatoes. There's a right way to do everything, and if you master those tricks, if you've got confidence in yourself, if you don't sweat the small stuff, you can cook anything. Moreover, you'll have a ball doing it—for the rest of your life.

Chapter 8

I will not eat oysters. I want my food dead. Not sick, not wounded, dead.

—*Woody Allen*

All summer long, I'd been eating lots of raw oysters. They went well with a dirty martini—something else I discovered during the project. There's such drama and ceremony involved in eating them that people forget how healthy oysters are. Oysters are high in protein, low in fat, contain omega-3 fatty acids, and are full of other minerals including iron, zinc, and copper. They're even a good source of vitamin B12. Lately, I'd gone overboard and ordered too many raw oysters. I was tired of eating them raw, but I still wanted to eat oysters.

One night in late May, we invited some folks over for a barbecue, and I planned to roast oysters out on the grill as the main protein. I hadn't cooked in a few weeks so I was enjoying thinking about what to make. But, as easy as grilling oysters is, I wanted to give it a test run before serving them to a crowd that would undoubtedly be disappointed to hear upon arriving that instead of steaks, ribs, sausages, hamburgers, or shrimp, they'd be sitting down to a pile of grilled oysters. Almost everyone (and definitely Brooke) would be thinking that I ruined what could have been a perfectly good evening. Until recently, had I shown up at someone's house for dinner and heard that we were eating oysters instead of—well anything else, I'd be ticked off, too. So if I was going to grill oysters, I had to make sure that people liked them.

Just before lunch, I headed out to shop for dinner. As usual, my basement office was freezing, but it was beautiful outside. I quickly checked out the garden we'd started in early March. It was growing well. We'd likely harvest a few cucumbers in the next day or two. They were getting huge, as were the early banana peppers. At dinner, Sasha would get a kick out of showing her friends all the beans we've got growing (purple, yellow, and green). I'd let the girls pick the mature beans themselves. They'd like that. Sasha loved the purple beans and had been sneaking out to the garden all week for samples. When I told her to go easy on them, she reminded me that they're healthy.

"Daddy. They're *beans.*"

"We won't have enough for an actual meal if we keep eating them out here in the garden."

"What's the difference?"

"I want us to cook them for you and Mommy."

"Romy likes beans too."

"Romy can have some beans."

"But she can't have the purple ones. They're just mine, right?"

"I think we can share the purple ones with your sister, don't you?"

"No. Not the purple ones. She doesn't like 'em. She's fine with the greens or the yellows. She likes them best."

"You quite sure about that?"

"Yeah. I know it, Dad."

Although she was totally full of it, watching her eat the purple beans right off the vine was a pleasure. She loved looking at the garden, and I loved watching her watch it. One morning, she secretly shoved a few purple beans in her pocket on the way to the park. She looked around to make sure the coast was clear and then subtly took a bite, doing her best to chew the beans without my noticing. It's nice being a kid.

After watering the garden and sneaking in a few beans myself, I drove up to Whole Foods and bought a dozen Wellfleet oysters. They weren't exactly cheap at $1.49 a pop, but they're delicious, and after all, this was an experiment. Wellfleet oysters are harvested from Wellfleet Harbor on the northeastern part of Cape Cod Bay. Wellfleet Harbor has a nutrient-rich mixture of fresh and saltwater, which is why this type of oyster is one of the most prized in the world. (Or so I read on Google.)

I bought a small tube of shallot and garlic compound butter. I hardly ever cooked with butter anymore, but it goes quite well with roast oysters. Plus, you only need a tiny amount, the size of a pea . . . maybe two, per oyster. You can easily substitute olive oil if you don't want to use butter. Slow roast some garlic on the stove over very low heat in a few fingers' worth of olive oil and whip them together with some sea salt and pepper before you put a bit on each oyster. That's delicious as well.

Grilling oysters is simple. When you have all the ingredients ready, including the butter or olive oil sauce, preheat your grill full blast. You want the grill screaming hot. I like to wash my oysters with a scrub brush in cold water just before I use them. Some folks say it's unnecessary but I think it helps get rid of some grit. Place the oysters directly on the grill flat side up so they're sitting in their liquor. Cover the grill and leave them alone. There's no need to rotate or flip them. Just let them cook until their shells pop open, which takes just a few minutes. Once the shells pop, they're ready to come off.

Take a serving plate and pour a healthy amount of sea salt, kosher salt, rice, or even lentils onto the platter so the oysters have a sturdy place to sit without rolling over. Plate the oysters and use a paring knife to pry the flat shell off the top. Some oysters will stick to the flat part of the shell, some will remain in their own little curved cup. Either way, you want to give each oyster a quick swipe with a knife between the meat and the shell so it's easier to eat. Once the top shells have been removed, take a small dollop of the compound butter and put it on top of each oyster. The residual heat from the shells will melt the butter.

Sasha is an incredibly adventurous eater, which makes us beam with pride. She ate two grilled oysters at the dinner. Two. I was impressed. As much as I grew up liking food, I surely wasn't eating oysters when I was four. Brooke and I sat there with our jaws on the ground as she coolly ate her first oyster as if it were a grape. When she reached for another one, Brooke whispered that we may have brought the wrong baby home from the hospital way back when.

The following week, Brooke and the girls left for a week in Maine with her family. I stayed in town to work. As is her wont, Brooke taped a note on the coffeemaker reminding me to pay the housekeeper, feed the cat, empty the litter box, change the lightbulb in the kitchen, take out the trash, pick up the dry cleaning, vote Democrat, and eat healthy in her absence. I intended to ignore everything on the list until Brooke called to tell me she was driving home from the airport, at which time I would scurry about the house frantically doing as I was told.

However, I did promise Brooke—and myself—that I'd eat healthy while she and the girls were gone. I wasn't nearly as keen on cleaning up after the cat. The dry cleaning could wait too. Personally, I work in sweatpants—a rare perk of this job.

Wanting to get off to a good start, I took a shower and headed for the grocery store as soon as the girls left. If I didn't bathe and get out of the house right away, I ran the risk of staying in bed all morning in a passively defiant celebration of having the house to myself.

I fully planned on keeping my healthy momentum going. The past four months found me in control of my appetite, my weight, my body, and my decisions about food. I hadn't been without sin, but I was on track and feeling healthy, maybe even a little fit. I even had a little bit of swagger—as much as I could muster after all those swaggerless years. Now I was a fruit-eating, veggie-loving, healthy-cooking, racquetball-playing, weight-lifting, water-drinking, badass motherfucker. I was going to stay on track that week. I had to. I wanted to. I honestly did. I wanted Brooke to come home the following week and notice that I looked better.

I headed up River Road to the Giant supermarket where I worked loading groceries into cars from the time I was fifteen until I went to college. It's the closest grocery store to my house. To say the least, I knew the way. Yet somehow, perhaps out of habit, I found myself making a left turn toward downtown Bethesda rather than straight up the hill to my Giant. I only snapped out of it and re- alized what I'd done once I was downtown. Instead of doubling back, I went to the store downtown instead.

Even though I was shopping for the entire week, I picked up far less than I planned, largely because most of the fruit was subpar. Their store-made grilled chicken salad, which had formed a large part of my diet for four months, also looked like it'd seen better days. I passed.

I was right up the street from Bradley Food and Bev- erage, a deli and gourmet food shop I've been going to since I was a kid. I love their turkey salad, so I figured I'd just drive over and get some of that instead of the sad- looking chicken salad. I'd also stop at the fruit stand on the way home and stock up on better produce. I'd be home before ten o'clock with a kitchen full of healthy choices to last me the better part of the week. Short of a few nights when I had dinner plans, I was looking good on the diet front. No bad food brought into the house, no bad food decisions to make. Shopping smart when you're on a diet is 90 percent of the game. If you shop healthy, you can't help but eat healthy at home.

I paid for my groceries at the Giant and drove the few blocks down to the shopping center where Bradley Food and Beverage is located. Then, in an instant, everything fell apart.

I told myself not to park where I'd have to walk past the bakery, Breads Unlimited. I parked there anyway, because I am an overconfident, self-sabotaging fool. Then, dancing that much closer to doom, I convinced myself that I had to stop at Strosniders Hardware just a few doors down from the bakery for . . . whatever. Now I was standing equidistant between the hardware store and the bakery. Without much arm twisting, I got myself to go inside and splurge on some bread for the turkey salad I was about to buy. I'd been going low carb for so long, a piece of bread sounded perfectly sinful. I knew I was lying about the piece of bread. I always lie to myself. It's my thing.

I was standing inside the bakery pretending to be there for challah. I felt like John Daly in a liquor store. I had no business standing there. I should have just left. I did not.

The smell of this particular bakery always reminds me of living in Spain. During the second semester of my junior year in college, I lived above a bakery in Grenada, Spain, that seemed to purposefully pump sweet aromas through the ventilation system. Even my clothes smelled like pastries. It was fantastic. I loved walking home, knowing that my tiny apartment would smell like fresh bread—no matter the time of day.

For six months I woke up to the smell of ensaïmadas—a Spanish pastry with a thin flaky crust, shaped into coils and topped with powdered sugar. This bakery was known for their ensaïmadas. In the mornings, locals would line up three deep, just below my window, eating ensaïmadas with hot chocolate or coffee. The hum and bustle of Spaniards ordering coffee and ensaïmadas was my alarm clock the entire time I lived in that apartment. Tough times.

By contrast, on this particular morning, I woke up at 6:15 to my screaming eighteen-month-old daughter, Romy, with a leaking poopy diaper. There was no pleasant scent of baked goods, nor the intoxicating grinding, tapping, and whooshing of Spanish baristas frantically trying to keep up with the morning rush. Today, there were only Pampers, baby wipes, snot, and Elmo before everyone ran off to Maine. My lazy Spanish mornings with a café con leche, a few ensaïmadas, and the *International Herald Tribune* had been replaced by a hurried cup of coffee and some oatmeal—both sans sugar. Spain was, once again, a foreign land. Even my memories seemed like someone else's.

I was jealous of the me who lived in Spain, who fell in love with two beautiful Dutch roommates at the same time, who had the world on a string. Where was that fellow now? He seemed to exist in another place and time. I barely recalled the man-child who studied overseas so long ago. These days, it's all I can do to remember to put on deodorant.

The love triangle with the Dutch girls seemed like something I read about in *Us Weekly*. Were they really as lovely as I remembered? I wonder what they'd make of me today? Would they even recognize my plump face? Would they run in horror from the bovine me? Are they still beautiful? Are they happy? In my mind, they haven't aged and they surely don't have mortgages or kids or gray hair or love handles or herniated discs or a constant, gnawing battle with anxiety. They live preserved in the magic of my dusty old memories—forever young.

Feeling like a charlatan, I stood in front of the bakery case, waiting for the cops or Alan Funt or that creepy guy from the *Cheaters* TV show to come busting through the door with cameras and crying family members—hysterical that they'd caught me in the act of being my true self. I was also waiting for the lady behind the counter to call my number—it was a busy Saturday morning. Regardless, I was breaking a promise to myself—and Brooke—yet again. All I wanted was some ripe fruit. How'd I end up there?

If you're not focused, you can lose it all in an instant.

"One treat," I told myself.

"Two," I responded.

"Okay, two. But you've got to go to the health club today. Promise?"

"I do. I'll even do an extra ten minutes of cardio, okay? Wanna stop being such a nudge?"

"I'm sorry."

"I forgive you."

I actually believed me, which was my first mistake. I have very honest eyes.

As I sized up the diet-busting options in the bakery case, I remembered that Phil was recently raving about their walnut danish ring. I'd never tried one, because it was big enough to bring to someone's house for brunch. It's not for one person. It could feed a dozen people, maybe more, if those dozen people didn't include Phil and me. The two of us could polish this thing off over an episode of *Meet the Press*. Yet before I had a chance to talk myself out of it, my number was called and I sheepishly ordered the walnut ring. I pondered making some aside about how I hoped my in-laws would like this at their crowded brunch party.

I was buying this huge danish ring, blowing my diet to smithereens, but ironically, I'd gotten nothing for the ride home. God forbid I make the four-minute drive without something to eat. I ordered myself a glazed cake doughnut shaped like a fortune cookie. It was still warm. Had I known, I'd have ordered two.

Walking out of the bakery, I was crushed. I could feel everything falling apart. It wasn't too late to fix this. I hadn't eaten anything yet. But I was too weak to stop myself. I was in charge, but absolutely out of control. I'd been here before, where I thought I had it all figured out only to see myself kick over my own sand castles.

I am my own worst enemy.

Unless I walked over to the trash can and threw the bakery bag away, I knew what was about to happen. I thought about throwing the bag away. I honestly did.

Instead, I put the bakery bag in the car and walked three doors down to Bradley Food and Beverage, where things went from bad to worse.

I've been eating Bradley's turkey salad since I was a kid. It's a simple recipe with nothing more than cubed turkey breast, mayonnaise, celery, and a few spices. I've convinced myself that it's not entirely unhealthy—save for the mayo. I made my way to the deli counter and ordered a medium container of turkey salad. *Normal.* I ordered a small container of sesame noodles. *Not on the diet but still manageable.* I ordered half a pound of mortadella. *Not good.* I ordered a half pound of coppa—sliced paper thin. *Bad.* Then I ordered a Reuben, with coleslaw instead of sauerkraut. *I'm going to hell.*

With a basketful of fattening food, I was ready to check out and head to my car where the walnut ring and donut are waiting. I had more than enough fat-guy food to guarantee the week would be a total disaster.

It got worse.

Bradley Food and Beverage had recently installed a small ice cream freezer right next to the checkout line. The freezer just happened to hold pints of Gifford's ice cream—the very same local favorite that I grew up eating. Making this fight even more lopsided, the flavors in the case were my absolute favorites: Swiss chocolate and vanilla bean. Of all the freezers in all the world . . .

Next thing I knew, I was putting a pint of each flavor in my basket. *Disaster.* Then, just as I was closing the freezer case, I saw an unfamiliar pint of Ben & Jerry's with the words "NEW, NEW, NEW" written on the lid.

Those of us who take our Ben & Jerry's seriously are always scanning the freezer case looking for the "new" or "limited batch" flavors that come out just a few times a year. The special flavors and new releases aren't always a home run (see: Egg Nog, Festivus, From Russia with Buzz, Grape Nut, Holy Cannoli, Hunka Burnin' Fudge, Jalapeño Lime, Lemon Peppermint Carob Chip, Miz Jelena's Sweet Potato Pie, Oh Pear, and Vermonty Python). Winner or not, I'd hate to think that a flavor came and went without my knowing it. It would be like missing a chance to see the circus passing through town.

I'd been eyeing this new flavor, Mission to Marzipan, for months. Until now, I'd been too focused on losing weight to try it. But the time had come. The package description read, "Sweet Cream Ice Cream with Almond Cookies & a Marzipan Swirl." *You had me at "sweet cream."* I added the third pint to my basket of shame and checked out. It was just before 10 AM and I was buying cold cuts, noodles, turkey salad, a Reuben, and three pints of ice cream. Brooke's plane hadn't even left the ground yet. Game over.

On the way home, I inhaled the cake doughnut in just a few bites. Not twenty minutes out of the oven, I imagine it was delicious. But I don't even remember eating it. I was going into that familiar dark place: binge mode. During a binge I don't taste and enjoy food as much as simply devour it so I can eat something else. I'm overpowered by my own weakness. I do things I don't want to do. I wanted to eat healthy and exercise while Brooke was gone. I left the house with every intention of doing so. An hour before, there was no way I was going to break the diet. It was impossible. So why had I just wolfed down a cake doughnut in my car? Why was I speeding home to eat a Reuben and a quarter of the walnut ring for breakfast? Why now? Why was I so weak?

I couldn't get inside the house fast enough. I was almost shaking as I unloaded the food. The anticipation was nearly sexual. It absolutely owned me. I put everything away except the Reuben and the walnut ring. They were staying with me. I unwrapped the greasy Reuben and put it on a large plate. I cut off a wedge of the walnut ring and put it on the same plate as the sandwich. Some coleslaw juice bled into the danish and was immediately soaked up. I couldn't have cared less. At this point, you could've thrown all this stuff in a blender and I'd have eaten it happily. I quickly headed up to our bedroom. I had the house to myself but still felt like being sequestered in the privacy of my room. I was at the front end of a full-blown meltdown. I was surprised I didn't just sit in the bathtub. I couldn't get far enough away from myself.

I pulled a large hand towel from the linen closet and lay it on the bed like a table cloth. It's not that I'm sophisticated. It's that I was scared to death that I'd spill Russian dressing on the comforter. Basically, I was scared of my wife. With my table set, I plopped down in bed, turned on CNN, and dug into the Reuben.

I have to say, they make a hell of a Reuben. It was damn good. The dressing and grease raced down my hands and fell like lipid water balloons, splattering onto the plate and towel. For a moment, I thought about eating just half the sandwich and saving the rest for later. The moment passed. No dice. A bender's a bender. I ate the whole sandwich and seamlessly moved to the walnut ring. I used the danish to sop up the little bits of corned beef and coleslaw. God forbid every morsel of food didn't end up in my mouth.

When I'm in a tailspin like this, it happens fast and it goes deep. It only ends when I'm ruined—too wasted or broke or full to keep it up. And, once I've crossed that line, the only thing that can stop me is running out of gas—whatever that gas might be.

To no one's surprise, I didn't go work out as I promised myself I would. Instead, I stayed in bed watching TV and waiting for my stomach to recover from what I'd just done. Once I stopped feeling bloated (about an hour later), I waddled down to the kitchen and took out the inch-thick stack of delivery menus we'd collected over the years. I knew what I was after, I just needed a phone number. When you fall off the wagon, you go to the things you know, the things you miss, the things you crave, the things you've sworn off. For me—that's Chinese food.

I decided to order from my local delivery place, Mei-wah. At this point, I was a food vampire. It was better to have something delivered to the house. I didn't want to be seen by someone I knew at a restaurant picking up takeout. I hadn't really had a full-on Chinese dinner since that day I went to meet Janet Zalman for the first time seven months before.

It seemed my diet may have caused a small recession

in the local Chinese delivery market. This is when you know your old eating habits were way out of whack.

"Hello, Meiwah, can I help you?"

"Order for delivery, please."

"Your phone number?"

"301-555-2801."

"Is your address 4808 Oak Street? Mr. Ugel, yes?"

"Yes. Correct."

"HELLO, MR. UGEL! We thought you *moved*."

"No, no—still here."

"Is everything okay? Still like Chinese food?"

"Yes. We still like Chinese food."

"Not sick?"

"No. I'm not sick."

"We are SO happy to hear that. Ready to order?"

"Yes."

"Thank God you're okay. We missed you."

"I missed you, too."

I really did miss them. I wasn't kidding. Neither were they.

I had two standard Meiwah orders—one when Brooke and the girls were home, and one for when I was alone and had little risk of getting caught. This was certainly looking like one of those nights. When it's just me, I tend to order nothing but appetizers. That night, at the feast of the binge eater, I ordered the following:

- Barbecued roast pork

- Deep-fried crispy Cornish hen

- Meat spring rolls

- Pan-fried meat dumplings

- Deep-fried salt-and-pepper shrimp

It was the usual delivery guy. When I opened the door, he practically hugged me. He was so happy to see me, it made me uncomfortable. He asked how my daughters were doing—I swear. Maybe he was just a shrewd businessman, because I gave him a 20 percent tip on the bill—thus guaranteeing many equally awkward interactions in the future when all I want is to eat my goddamn dumplings and be left alone.

Meiwah insists on tying your plastic bag in a "creative" knot that allows you to carry the bag with one big loop. Admittedly, it works well as a handle. Unfortunately, there's no way to untie the bag no matter how you twist and pull—or use your teeth. It's degrading to sit there trying to break into your own dinner. With way too much anger behind it, I went at the bag with a pair of kitchen scissors. Take that, China.

I unpacked the bag and lined up the black rectangular boxes in a nice, neat row—removing their lids one by one as if working on an assembly line. The slightest bit of steam rose from the boxes as I removed their tops. I took two serving platters from the cabinet and loaded the different dishes on top.

Sitting in the lotus position on the sofa in the living room, I pulled the coffee table close to me and began. I dipped a crispy dumpling in soy and rice-wine vinegar sauce. The dumplings weren't too doughy. They were full of spicy meat, still juicy and hot. The roast pork was good tonight. There were plenty of end pieces—my favorite part. The wok-fried shrimp were topped with a crispy mélange of minced ginger, garlic, and spicy Chinese pepper. Wonderful.

The deep-fried Cornish hen is, perhaps, their best dish. The hen comes with its own dipping sauce—far less intense than the vinegar-based dumpling sauce. This one is more akin to the subtle sauce served with tempura—almost an au jus. The bird's skin and little end pieces get perfectly crunchy as they remain in the fryer until just this side of overcooked. Cooking the small bird in this manner almost invariably leaves the breast meat dry and boring. I tend to pawn off the breasts to Brooke and the girls in favor of the sublime thighs, tiny legs, wings, and back portion, which are practically nothing but crispy hen-flavored chips.

Then, of course there's the bird's tush—"the pope's nose," as my dad calls it. For the vast majority of my life I watched in horror as my dad and older sister, Niki, would fight over who got to eat the chicken's ass.

Dad and Niki were always trying things the rest of us wouldn't eat on a bet—blood sausage, headcheese, sweetbreads, fish eyeballs, sea urchin, chicken livers, shad roe, tongue, chicken feet, tripe, calf brains, the occasional lamb testicle. There was, however, something about watching Dad and Niki chew on a chicken's ass that just killed me. It seemed demonic and, not to mention, entirely unsanitary. I was obsessed with the notion that the last bit of chicken poop was still trapped in the bird's tush. They *had* to be eating chicken shit. I saw no evidence to the contrary. I watched my sister willingly eat chicken ass and felt sad for her, as if it were a cry for help—perhaps a last ditch attempt to win our father's attention. *Look Dad, I love eating bird ass, too! Please, love me.* It made snacking on a lamb's testicle seem downright normal.

Little did I know that she and Dad were onto something—crazy like a couple of foxes. The chicken's tail is nothing but fat and skin divided by a small row of bones. As it cooks, the tail becomes crispy and delicious. They weren't insane (at least not about that). They were likely thrilled that the rest of us turned our heads in horror as they sat there nibbling on the best bit of the bird. Today, I too seek out bird butts. Brooke looks at me with the same disgust I felt toward Dad and Niki way back when. She doesn't know what she's missing. Honey, please pass the tushy. . . .

For a few minutes there on the sofa, while I was immersed in thoughts of food and enjoying my meal, the disappointment in myself faded away. I was, once again, alone with my old friend. The scale, the diet, Janet, Brooke, David—they all went away. It was just me and my Chinese food—no judgments, no broken promises, no excuses—that would all be there waiting for me . . . when I was full. Now it was time to be high. It was intense, and over in just a few moments. Perhaps that's why a binge is so great—because this feeling doesn't last. It ends and real life comes back into focus.

There were leftovers, just a few, but I didn't keep them. I threw everything out in an attempt to both cover my tracks if my mother-in-law stopped by and to absolve myself of the sin. If there were no leftovers in the fridge, it had never happened. Out of sight, out of mind. I actually took the trash bag out to the cans on the side of the house where the raccoons would try to get at the bones and scraps. Let *them* eat the dried-out breast meat. With the evidence out of the house, I could start fresh, begin anew—pretend this away. Even though I was all alone, I was still covering my tracks, hiding my addiction from everyone save for the raccoons who live in the sewer. They, like me, will eat anything they can get their hands on. They, like me, will do anything to get some food that they should not eat. They, like me, are more than willing to eat trash.

Not an hour after all that Chinese food, I was back in the freezer collecting what remained of my ice cream. I blame the MSG. There was a pint and a half left over from that morning. I sat right there in the kitchen and finished it off. A pint and a half—gone in maybe ten minutes. The Mission to Marzipan was good—if a little too sweet for my taste. My wife and daughters had been gone for roughly twelve hours. In that time I'd eaten three pints of ice cream, a Reuben, half a walnut ring, and forty dollars' worth of Chinese food. There were five more days until their return. Five days. Enough time to ruin everything.

I caught an unexpected break the following morning. I got on the scale expecting to weigh at least a pound, if not two, more than yesterday. Instead, the scale showed that I weighed exactly what I had the previous morning. How was that possible? I had no earthly idea. How could I have eaten everything I did yesterday and not have it show up on the scale?

The scale is weird like that. This wasn't the first time I'd been surprised by the number that the digital display settled on after a day when I went off course. I think it shows that your body reacts to and processes food differently if you've been eating healthy and exercising on a regular basis versus times when you've consistently eaten poorly and not worked out. As bad as yesterday was, I'd been eating well for months. I was exercising almost every day. My body is a lot more forgiving when I'm taking care of it. Maybe my metabolism is actually responding to all the work at the gym? Maybe I'd just dodged a bullet, even though I shot the gun at myself.

I'd somehow earned a mulligan, a do-over. From the scale in my bathroom, down the stairs to the main floor, and the ten steps to the kitchen, I was born again. I could regroup, stop hating myself, untie the knot that had been in my stomach since yesterday, and get back to the business of being healthy. Apparently, the new me was still here. I had just taken a day off to go nuts. Okay. Fair enough. Apology accepted. Lesson learned. Back on the horse. Whew . . . that was close.

I was off the hook that I swallowed yesterday. I was so relieved, I all but moonwalked into the kitchen. I started to make coffee. I reached to my right for a banana but my hand landed on a white bakery box—the walnut ring.

I hadn't thrown away the leftover danish along with

the Chinese food. There was half a walnut ring sitting right there. The coffeemaker bubbled and hissed—reminding me of the obvious. Coffee and a walnut ring are a perfect match. I begged myself to throw it out. Start the day right. Get back on track. Better yet, I told myself to run the pastry under the faucet first so I wouldn't go get it out of the trash—something I'm absolutely not above doing. I took the ring to the sink and opened the box. As I was turning on the water, I noticed that one section of the Danish was overloaded with icing and nut clusters. I saw this very same piece last night and thought it was out of character for me not to eat it first. It was clearly the prized piece on the whole ring. It was the oyster on the chicken thigh, the end cut on a prime rib, the cap on a rib-eye steak. Who or what was I saving it for?

I was saving it for this morning.

Like a zombie, I turned the water off and put the box on the kitchen island. I took out a knife and cut another quarter piece of the walnut ring (the third of four). I put it in the microwave for twenty seconds, got my cup of coffee, grabbed a fork, and headed upstairs to the purgatory of my bedroom. I wanted to eat in peace.

It'd been three minutes and I was off the wagon . . . again.

The thrill of the scale was short-lived. I felt powerless to say no to the pastry once I saw it. It was as if the decision were already made—preordained. The diet never had a chance. If there had been no pastry in the kitchen, would I have driven back to the bakery and bought another one? Absolutely not. But the sight of the walnut

ring seemed to cause a chemical reaction in my brain elic-
iting an overpoweringly strong emotional response. As
David Kessler says in his book, *The End of Overeating,* "Rewarding foods tend to be reinforcing, meaning they keep
us coming back for more."[7] Moreover, the white bakery
box, almost iconic in its easily recognizable form, trig-
gered a Pavlovian response in the pleasure center of my
brain. White box equals sweet, fat, sugary, baked food.
The box didn't "make me do it," but it surely didn't help.

While the flavors and ingredients of certain foods
(specifically sugar, fat, and salt) are fundamental to our
brain's receptors, the emotional response to various foods
is equally powerful—sometimes even more powerful—
than the flavors and ingredients themselves. Kessler describes the dynamic like this:

> Cues associated with the pleasure response
> demand our attention, motivate our behavior,
> and stimulate the urge we call "wanting." When
> those cues are present, we learn to pursue food
> with greater vigor to secure the expected reward.
> With experience, the association between cues
> and food becomes even stronger, and we be-
> come more single-minded in our focus and our
> pursuit. That increases consumption. We pursue
> the food more frequently, and the resulting
> pleasure leads us to repeat the behavior. A

7. David A. Kessler, *The End of Overeating* (New York: Rodale
Press, 2009)

continuous cycle of cue-urge-reward is set in motion and eventually becomes a habit.[8]

Once I ate the walnut ring, everything really fell apart. At 10:35 AM, I did the unthinkable. I drove to McDonald's—the dieter's equivalent of waving the white flag. I officially and unequivocally surrendered. However, just as I pulled into the drive-thru, I realized that I'd arrived during their ambiguous 10:30 AM to 11 AM half hour just after breakfast and just before lunch during which they don't really have anything to offer except for leftover Egg McMuffins. Technically they're serving lunch, but everything's in flux and it's best to just wait it out till 11 AM.

Determined not to be the fat guy in the drive-thru willing to eat their leftovers, I backed my car into a corner of the parking lot, turned up the West Coast feed of Howard Stern on satellite radio, and waited.

I'd hit rock bottom.

I was waiting for the clock to strike 11 AM so I could have a Filet-O-Fish. Pathetic. That's why I was hiding in the corner of the parking lot. Try explaining this to, well, anyone who stumbles by. If you're just randomly sitting in a McDonald's parking lot at this hour, you're either waiting for lunch to start or meeting someone to buy weed.

I'd lost forty-one pounds. I had only nine to go. Yet the second my wife left town, I started acting like a pris-

---

8. David A. Kessler, *The End of Overeating* (New York: Rodale Press, 2009)

oner on a conjugal visit. Not to mention, there were far more interesting ways to break a diet than going to McDonald's. How pedestrian. If I was going to go off the reservation, why not hit Ruan Thai for some duck? I could call Phil and see if he's in the mood for dim sum. I could find my way to Houston's for a rack of ribs, maybe drive to that Korean place in Virginia for some barbecued pork belly. Why was I here? I was supposed to be a foodie. What gives?

McDonald's is both fast (this moment notwithstanding), and somewhat infamous for their role in the obesity epidemic our country faces. If you want to mainline food that will wipe your diet off the face of the earth, and you want to do it in a hurry—without even getting out of the car—this is the place to come.

Is that totally fair to the McDonald's corporation, which has been trying like hell to change the public's perception of their food since Morgan Spurlock's documentary *Super Size Me*? Probably not. I'm sure they're crying all the way to the bank. Just that week, while I was breaking my diet, Wall Street had announced that McDonald's profits were up—in part due to their new "coffee bars," where you can get one of three different drinks: cappuccino, mocha, or latte. Their attempt to challenge Starbucks and other coffeehouses for a larger piece of the massive coffee market has been a success. Of course, they're not after the high-end coffee drinkers who want their half-caf-skim-soy-Macchiato with extra foam. Try ordering *that* at McDonald's. They'll stab you with a plastic spork.

More than anything, the new McDonald's espresso-based offerings all have one thing in common—sugar. McDonald's has created an ingenious new sugar delivery system, masquerading as a coffee bar. That's why they're selling a lot of these new drinks. Folks want their sugar—even if they think they're really after caffeine. Why are profits up at McDonald's? It's the sugar, stupid.

McDonald's has positioned itself as a one-stop shop for sugar, fat, and salt—the triumvirate of our obesity epidemic. They give us what our increasingly contaminated bodies demand. They are drug dealers in corporate costumes. And while their drugs are legal, the chain's impact on our culture has been as devastating as crack or meth. Behind Ronald McDonald's rosy smile is a scary clown dragging us further down the drain with every Happy Meal, Big Mac, Filet-O-Fish, Quarter Pounder, french fry, icy Coke, thick shake, sundae, and apple pie they sell.

At the top of the hour, I pulled into the drive-thru lane and ordered a Filet-O-Fish, a Big Mac, six Chicken McNuggets, and a chocolate shake. This was bad. Even worse, it was totally premeditated. I can't blame impulse. I sat here in the parking lot for twenty minutes waiting for them to start serving lunch. I had more than enough time to rethink the decision and retreat. Instead, I spent all that time debating whether to order a Quarter Pounder or a Big Mac—similar to how Thoreau passed the hours on Walden Pond.

Brooke and I have done surprisingly well keeping the kids away from McDonald's. Sasha still calls it "Old Mac-Donald's," so unfamiliar with the restaurant that she's convinced it has something to do with the children's song. Whatever works. Soon enough, she, like every other child in our country, will know the place all too well. For now, I'd much rather she think *E-I-E-I-O,* than french fries and Happy Meals as we drive past.

Historically, I've rarely eaten at McDonald's, much less ordered a Big Mac. I'm not quite sure why I ordered it that day. Perhaps it was the decadence of the thing— three pieces of bread, *two all beef patties, special sauce, lettuce, cheese, pickles, onions, on a sesame bun.* Ordering a Big Mac was a way of punishing myself for the appetites in my head. You want McDonald's, fat boy? You wanna blow your diet? You need your dose of fat and salt? You want to eat a burger made from hundreds of different cows? You can't keep your shit together for one day without your wife here to watch you like a fifth grader? You want to be bad? You got it. *Eat this.*

I ate the six nuggets on the three-minute drive back to my house. Nuggets rarely last beyond the car ride home. At the house, I sat down to polish off the rest of the food while watching Drew Carey on *The Price Is Right.* Trying to keep some semblance of regard for my well-being, I pulled the middle piece of bread out of the Big Mac and threw it away—but not before licking the "special sauce" and minced onions off the bun. Not eating the middle piece of bread is akin to sweeping up some dust at a garbage dump.

Brooke called just as I was shoving the last of the Big Mac into my mouth. I watched my cell phone ring and vibrate on the table—deciding whether or not to answer it. It was my wife. We hadn't spoken in a day. I couldn't remember the last time we'd gone that long without speaking. She was in Deer Isle, Maine, which gets the worst cell reception of anywhere I've ever visited in the country. She was likely standing on her tippy toes at the top of some hill, hoping that the weak signal would stay put until she could say hello to her husband. Maybe she had the girls there? Maybe they missed me? Maybe they just wanted to say, "I love you" to Daddy? Or maybe something was wrong?

There were a thousand reasons to pick up the phone. There was only one reason not to. My mouth was full of Big Mac, and I was ashamed of myself. When I'm like this, I don't want to speak to anyone, much less Brooke and the girls. I'm alone in body and mind. Talking to the girls right then would have introduced their characters into this odd scene. I couldn't deal. I let the phone ring for the fifth and final time. I just sat there chewing and waiting for the red light to start blinking, indicating that I had a voice mail. Within a minute or so the light started flashing.

Shame. . . . shame. . . . shame. . . . shame. . . . shame. . . . shame. . . . shame. . . . shame.

Grudgingly, I pressed the voice-mail button with my pinky finger—the only digit not covered in special sauce. I put the phone on speaker. The signal was weak and scratchy. But the message hit me right in the face.

"Hi, Honey. I can't believe I got a signal. We're fine. Long drive from the airport yesterday. The girls were just so-so. Romy slept for a bit, which was great. Sasha was in rare form.

Tantrum city. We all miss you. I bet you're playing racquetball with Skipper or working out with David. (Ouch!) I hope you're doing well on the diet. I'm proud of you. (Ouch!) You can do this, baby. Just stay focused. (Kill me.) I love you. . . . Hold on, Sasha wants to say hi . . .

. . . Hi Daddy! We just went blueberry picking by the water. Romy ate so many that her tongue turned BLUE! She didn't like to pick 'em so she just ate mine. I shared really well. I miss you. Maybe you can have some cucumbers from the garden? I left you some beans too, remember? Did you pick them yet? Did you water the garden? Is it raining there? Do you like snow cones? We had 'em after lunch. We ate ribs, too. Okay, love you, Daddy. Bye.

For the second time that day, I thought about starting fresh. For the second time that day, I didn't listen to myself. I sat there in a food coma, watching the Showcase Showdown, feeling like a pig. I didn't move for hours. When I finally peeled myself off the couch, it was nearly three o'clock. I got back in the car and headed to another old stomping ground, the Wow Cow ice cream parlor just a few minutes from my house—across the street from McDonald's.

Wow Cow is a place for my compulsive eating and insane, nearly pathological insecurity to come stare at each other.

"So . . . how ya been?"

"You know, same old, same old."

"You look good."

"Thank you. No I don't, but—thank you. You too . . . you too . . . I should really, um, I should really get going."

"Yeah, me too. Very busy myself. I've got a thing . . . downtown."

I hadn't been to Wow Cow in the better part of a year. Since my last visit, I'd lost forty-one pounds. Still, I walked in hoping that it was a different girl behind the counter. It was not. It was the same cute girl, plus another one either working or sent there by my shrink to fuck with me. My need for ice cream outweighed my discomfort. I was a chubby thirty-seven-year-old married man with two children, gray hair, and a bad back. Goddamnit, I wanted some ice cream.

The girl recognized me. Before I could tell her what I wanted—she told me. She remembered my order: a quart of Oreo and a pint with half coconut and half black raspberry. I was not flattered. This wasn't some sexy barista who knew I liked a small Americano at the coffee shop. This was a kid I hadn't seen in a year who remembered how much ice cream I eat. And I think we just answered the question of how much better I looked after dropping forty-one pounds. Apparently, I was still me.

Waiting for her to scoop my ice cream felt like an eternity. There was nothing to do but sit there. Time stood still. There was no one else in the shop, and aside from the hum of the freezers, you could hear a pin drop. Making matters worse, her coworker was just standing there staring at me. She was chewing gum and blowing bubbles. I was too intimidated to look directly at her, but I could see her in the mirror behind the counter. Oh, she was looking.

The scooper asked me if I wanted a spoon. Did I want a spoon for the quart and a half of ice cream I just ordered? Did she actually think there was a chance I might just sit in the car and eat it right now? (Don't answer that.) Did she ask everyone this question or just fatties? Was there a certain amount of ice cream at which point she realized that the customer was more than likely taking it home? Humiliating.

Over the next twenty-four hours, I ate both the quart of Oreo and the pint of coconut and black raspberry. It got to the point where I wasn't even tasting the flavor anymore. I was simply filling up the hole in myself, one bowl at a time. I couldn't believe that I could actually fit all that ice cream into my body. I felt my stomach expanding. I felt myself gaining weight.

I slept the day away. I woke up at odd hours and mindlessly headed to the freezer for another bowl of ice cream. I wouldn't stop until it was gone. I couldn't do anything other than eat it or think about eating it or think about how awful it was that I was eating it.

The time alone was my very own food festival. I covered most of the places I hadn't been eating during those days—Thai, Korean, dim sum, Chinese, Popeye's. In a day, my family would be home, and I'd stop eating like this. I wanted to stop sooner, but I didn't. If I really wanted to, I would have. I refused to get it together. I was eating. And, I hated myself for eating. It was all I thought about, and all I did.

In the aftermath of the girls' trip to Maine, I ate like a fiend for three weeks. I was totally off course. I gained back five pounds. I canceled three of my weekly appointments with Janet—lying to her that I was away on vacation. I didn't have the nerve to face David and let him see me. He has such a good eye, he'd know that I'd put on weight.

My choices had consequences. I'd set the project back a month. That's how long it was going to take to lose the weight I put on over those few weeks. I was going to be paying off this food tab for a while.

Minor decisions can have a considerable impact on your life. I had no intention of buying ice cream, or going to that goddamn bakery in the first place. I stumbled into an opportunity to fail or succeed—a test. I failed. Was it a simple twist of fate? Did I knowingly set it up to sabotage myself? Am I that afraid of success?

I'm not a big believer in fate. I have a hard time wrapping my head around the idea that my life, my successes, and my mistakes aren't my own. Still, I was thinking about fate the whole time the girls were away. What if I hadn't made that left turn on the way to the market the other day? What if I'd ended up at my usual Giant instead? What if the chicken salad at the store had been fresh and appetizing? What if I never went to the other shopping center to get turkey salad? What if I never saw the small freezer by the cashier? Would I still have ended up with three pints of ice cream in my basket? I'll never know for sure. I am, however, struck with the randomness of it all—how one bad decision can snowball into something larger than you can control.

Fate didn't cause that crazy week to transpire. I did. Still, I'm humbled by how quickly my lesser self came to the surface. The second I gave myself an opportunity to fail, I failed. It all happened so fast. While I was the one making all the decisions, it sure took me by surprise how reckless I was. I made the decision to crack a window and all my demons came racing through with the wind. Oops.

I understand addiction more than I ever thought I would. Sometimes, the tail wags the dog. Moreover, you could go back and reread the past thirty pages of this book and replace *food* with *cocaine, alcohol, sex,* or *gambling* and have a pretty good idea how the mind of an addict works. That's tough to say but true. I don't think I could have admitted that six months ago. I was too busy calling myself a foodie to realize that I'm a food addict and compulsive eater first, and a foodie a distant second.

What was the lesson? For one thing, you can't take your eye off the ball. You make choices all the time, and you'd better have your act together when you do, because those seemingly minor decisions matter—a lot. Also, don't forget who you really are. I should have known better than to play around as if I had everything under control. I have nothing under control. I rarely do.

I also got too wrapped up in all the noise surrounding the diet. I didn't learn to live in the silence—when it was just me—no scale, nothing to prove. At times over the year, I exercised and ate right. But there was always an elephant in the room. What was going to happen when I was all alone? What would happen when the project was done and there was nothing riding on my health except . . . my health? Could I live a healthy lifestyle for myself?

My mother-in-law, Karen, is a yoga teacher. She talks about certain folks who just can't handle the intensity, the absolute quiet, the look inward, that yoga demands. Some people can exercise like madmen every day, but they just can't take the silence of yoga. It's too scary to be that intimate, that quiet with themselves. I think that's been me this year and maybe my entire life. With an audience—be they a reader, my wife, my family, my friends . . . anyone who knew about the diet—I've largely been able to walk the walk. I've acted like a healthy person, in control of his choices. Once the project ends, I have to work on living in the silence, in the quiet of my mind—not exactly a place known for its serenity.

What is it in me that finds it so easy to fail and so hard to succeed? As I got closer to my goal weight, I somehow started to believe less and less that I would succeed. How was that possible? Why, when I had fifty pounds to lose, did I jump in and believe that I could lose that much weight, and then become so full of self-doubt with just under ten pounds to go? I couldn't make heads or tails of it. Was I afraid of success? Did I want to fail? Was I just lazy? Did I simply tire out after so many months of being good to my body?

Why do I eat like this? What am I feeding? Why do I feel empty? I still don't know. I eat all the time. I eat when I'm happy, sad, stressed, relaxed, depressed, mad, proud, nervous, calm. I eat to punish myself. I eat to reward myself. I love eating. I love cooking. I love watching people cook. I love watching people eat. I love reading about food. I love writing about food. I love thinking about food. It's my hobby, my passion, my life.

So many of my happiest times have been directly or indirectly related to food. Food is my identity. When I cook for people, that's how I show them love. If I cook for you, I'm wooing you. That's how I make myself available to people, because I'm a socially awkward, introverted mess. I need to cook, because it's one of the few things I'm good at doing that makes people happy.

Brooke thinks I need to understand that an all-encompassing passion for food is dangerous for me. She believes my love of food will kill me if I go on like this. She's right. But she doesn't love food the way I do. She loves eating great food—but not like me. Take away my cooking shows, my shopping trips to the specialty market, my cooking with Sasha and Romy, and I feel less whole, less interesting, less interested. Yes, I have to find a way to put food in perspective in my life. But I'm desperate to do so without walking away from the kitchen.

In the meantime, there was only one way to stop spinning. I set up another week on the BluePrintCleanse. I dreaded the green juice, but I couldn't wait to start over. Punishment comes in all shapes and sizes.

Chapter 9

Find the shortest, simplest way between the earth, the hands, and the mouth.

—*Lanza del Vasto*

It was June. My friend Marco was getting married in New Orleans, and I was just two short months away from the project deadline. After gaining those five pounds while Brooke and the girls were in Maine and during the weeks afterward, I'd lost thirty-seven pounds altogether. With thirteen pounds to go, both the goal and the deadline were in sight. To say the least, a wild wedding weekend in the Big Easy was a dangerous proposition.

As luck would have it, nearly all our wives were staying home because of pregnancies, young kids, or both. Cue the sad music. A few guys were coming down with their wives. The rest of us would just have to survive on our own. However would we manage?

What I was really looking at was a long weekend in one of my favorite cities, surrounded by my best foodie friends—with no one to tell me to put down the étouffée. Think *Caligula* starring a bunch of chubby, balding Jews.

Diet? That weekend? In New Orleans? Define *diet*. I was merely planning to survive. My goal was simple: not to come back fatter than when I left. I was obviously not going to lose weight down there. I'd likely gain a pound simply printing out my boarding pass. New Orleans on a diet is like Vegas with no cash—it stinks.

On the plus side, I'd be walking all over the city, especially with the clowns I call my friends. You've never met a group of lazier guys in your life. This crew would take a cab to the bathroom if they could pull it off. But for some reason, my friends love walking in New Orleans. Is it to help burn off a few po' boys? No. I think they're inclined to walk because of the city's "to-go" alcohol policy. Anyone of age can walk the streets with a cocktail or beer in their hands. Yes, it's kind of cool. But just because you can drink a beer while walking through the French Quarter doesn't make a thirty block schlep any less annoying. Not to mention that I'm a bit of a sweater. I'm also lugging around a bunch of extra fat. A long walk in schvitzy New Orleans leaves Fatty with that not-so-fresh feeling. I've got enough problems looking presentable without doing a 5K just to reach a bar. I don't exactly give off that James Bond vibe as I waddle through the doors complaining of chafed inner thighs. How many times that weekend was I going to hear someone tell me, "It's just a few more blocks"? My kingdom for a cab and some Vaseline.

When I'm in New Orleans, I end up eating the same seafood (oysters, shrimp, soft-shell crabs, and catfish) that I love up in Maryland. We like what we like. I appreciate classic New Orleans cuisine. But after all this time, I still don't understand the fuss over étouffée, gumbo, and jambalaya. To me they're always too something—too salty, too many competing ingredients, too much stuff thrown into one pot. All three dishes are just too busy for me. While I always want a bite or two of someone else's, I'd only order these dishes if the other menu options were vegan.

I find the real difference between eating in Maryland and Louisiana is that in New Orleans, you're more likely to have friends hurrying you through dinner so they can continue partying like they're in Amsterdam. That's really what New Orleans is—America's Amsterdam—with less weed and better music. The vibe in the streets, the palpable sense of chaos, the nonstop party—that's New Orleans. In New Orleans you're always keenly aware that no matter what you're doing, there is undoubtedly someone within a block doing something a lot worse. It's titillating to know that there's all kinds of odd behavior going on nearby, no matter what part of town you're in. I'm a fan of the naughtiness.

Unfortunately, New Orleans attracts more fools than a Ponzi scheme. Bourbon Street and the blocks that surround it are as close to my version and understanding of hell as you can get. There are two types of tourists who come to New Orleans: those who can't wait to get to Bourbon Street, and those who avoid it like the tourist pit that it is. Are the drunk, belligerent fools found only on Bourbon Street? No, but I strongly believe they consider Bourbon Street home base.

There are four things I love about New Orleans. First,

it's one of the best food towns in the United States. If you know where to go, both the lowbrow and the high-end cuisine are superb. There's no shortage of new and interesting places to try, even after vital parts of the city were gutted by Hurricane Katrina. Every joint has its own take on the local classics. There are different preparations of the same dish all over town. Isn't a gumbo a gumbo? Hardly. Try telling that to the local cooks and proprietors who swear their house recipe is *the* standard by which all others should be judged. If you want to be a good guest, it's only fair to try as many versions as possible so no one feels left out.

Second, the city's music scene is unparalleled. It's the one town in the world where a homebody like me is liable to see the sun rise while listening to live music. Is music a big part of my life? Sometimes. However, many of my friends are serious music junkies. To them, New Orleans is akin to visiting Mecca. They know who's playing in town weeks before we arrive. Thus, when I'm in New Orleans with these guys, I'm a music freak too. When in Rome.

Third, there's the booze. Like everyone else in town, I tie on a good buzz in New Orleans. Vodka flows like water. But I've never had a "hurricane" or any other ridiculous tourist drink served in a tall plastic cup that looks exactly like the bong I had in college. Sadly, the sight of frat boys stumbling down Bourbon Street with pink souvenir cups half-full of melted, frozen crap is a way of life in New Orleans. Like mosquitoes at the beach, it's the price you pay for being there. Why can't these kids be classy like me and drink dirty martinis until they can't see straight? I weep for our future.

Finally, there's gambling. Harrah's casino, which opened in 1999, sits right between the French Quarter and the mighty Mississippi River. That way, when you lose your shirt at the craps tables, it's a convenient walk to go drown yourself. Harrah's is also a stone's throw from all the main hotels . . . including the one I'll be staying in for the wedding.

For years I'd do anything in order to gamble. Over the past few years, I stopped gambling and started eating with the same addictive gusto. The power of the two addictions is similar. All addicts have the same stories, regardless of their background. Ever since I accepted the fact that I'm a food addict, I see that food addiction is no different from gambling or any other addiction. When you lose control, addictions take you to some unhealthy, unholy, unhappy places.

Being a food lover doesn't automatically make you a food addict. Being a food addict doesn't necessarily mean that you can't be a foodie. When I'm cooking a meal for my friends or family—I'm a foodie. When I have a leftover lamb shank in one hand and birthday cake in the other at six thirty in the morning—I'm an addict.

For most of my life I thought I was just a proper foodie, until I looked back and recalled the countless times I'd found myself polishing off a quart of ice cream in one sitting. Foodies don't need a half gallon of Oreo ice cream . . . ever. No one does. But a food addict, *this* food addict, can destroy that much ice cream without so much as blinking. And, as with my worst casino moments—I didn't even feel it as it was happening. I was numb to it. It's only afterward, when the demons are fed, that you grasp what you've allowed yourself to do. But in the moment, the rest of your brain just shuts down, obedient to the voice inside you, allowing you to do things you know you'll regret.

Within hours I'd be in New Orleans. I was supposedly a newer, cleaner, thinner version of the man who used to make such banal, selfish choices back in the day. Yes, I'd lost nearly forty pounds, but I still had plenty of demons to keep at bay that weekend. I had a list of food to avoid while I was in New Orleans. It was just a matter of prioritizing. More than anything else, I kept thinking about the beignets. There's nothing like walking into the French Quarter and sitting down in a café for a coffee and a few beignets. Would I be able to say no? Was I going to watch my friends eat beignets while I just sat there? Did I have that kind of willpower? Could I stay away from all the fried food? What about bread? How can you eat a po' boy if you're avoiding bread? What about the pralines? What's New Orleans without all the food?

With all the restrictions on what I could eat, this was feeling more like a trip to Mars than New Orleans. Without the food, what was left to do? Who would I be in that town without the things that make the Big Easy so much fun? Who was I when I wasn't eating?

Before I faced my demons down there, I had to pack. The history of my weight struggle was evident in what was going on in my closet. When you've gained—and then lost—so much weight so quickly, packing for a wedding weekend is a nightmare. Nothing fits. It was hard to remember which suits I had tailored to fit my girth and which ones were patiently waiting for me to get my act together before I could even think about wearing them again. Dreading the results, I tried on all the suits in my closet—one by one—then hung them back up. Nothing fit. I had these beautiful Canali suits that I hadn't worn in years. The entire collection was worth more than my car. It was a demoralizing exercise.

At my current weight, I had no clue what fit. Most of my fat suits were now too big. I was swimming in one of them. On the one hand, that was great news. There's nothing like getting too thin for your fat clothes. But I had to fit into *something* for this damn wedding. I was in clothes purgatory.

Still between sizes, I reluctantly brought one of my fat-guy suits down to Louisiana. Thirty-seven pounds lighter and I was still in a suit from the Big and Tall store. Depressing. I was going to wear the fat suit even though it made me look like the kid in the final scene of *Big*. One of my smaller suits fit, but it was still too snug—especially for a long, hot New Orleans wedding night. The snug pants would remind me not to overeat, but I definitely wouldn't have as much fun. No matter what I wore, I still looked doughy. What's the old saying about putting lipstick on a pig? I was down a few sizes—and a few belt notches. But, the truth is, I was still a puffy mess. There wasn't a suit in the world that could save me that weekend.

Many of my closest friends would be at the wedding.

Sadly, I rarely saw them these days. A lot of them still lived in Portland, Oregon, as I did for four years in the mid-'90s. When I lived in Portland, I was thinner . . . a lot thinner. I weighed between 185 and 190. Even though I'd now lost thirty-seven pounds, showing up in New Orleans weighing 226 pounds wasn't going to impress anybody. I was just hoping nobody would gasp in horror. No matter what I weighed, my friend Jason would have a notebook full of fat jokes waiting for me when I arrived. I could show up looking like Christian Bale in *The Machinist,* and within minutes he'd have me near tears. The guy knows how to hit a nerve, which is why he's funny. I don't know why he's short.

At the airport, I was full of nervous energy. I was excited to see everyone. I was also getting worried about falling off the health wagon. I did have a game plan. Janet and I had talked about how I should try to eat and what to avoid. But I was anxious about the entire trip. Plus, I was about to board a plane. I'm not a great flyer. Years ago, I had a terrible flight returning from a business trip to Nashville. Lightning was bouncing our plane around like a basketball. People were holding hands and praying— even I was praying. Ever since, I take a pill to help me relax when I fly. It tends to work. Still, when we hit turbulence, I'll squeeze Brooke's thigh until she's nearly in tears. She's such a baby.

The flight down to New Orleans was not without incident. The pill I took knocked me out. I'm sure it had nothing to do with the martini I used to wash it down before the flight. The pill-martini combo worked a little too well; I woke myself up somewhere over Mississippi with what I can only describe as a humiliating snore-fart. Just as startled as everyone else, I opened my eyes and saw three rows of bewildered passengers glaring at me in disgust. There's very little room for recovery after you do that. You just sit there, completely mortified. I considered whacking my head and demanding to watch *People's Court* so folks would feel sorry for me. Instead, I buried my nose in a copy of the *New Yorker* hoping that everyone would think me too intellectual to have quite possibly shit in my own pants at 32,000 feet.

I arrived at the International House Hotel, where my friend Uri has already checked in and left me a key at the desk. Uri is a perfect guy to knock around with in New Orleans. A classically trained chef and successful restaurateur, he's got a nose for little hole-in-the-wall joints, well off most tourists' radar. While I was there, I planned to follow him around like a puppy, eating where and what he told me to. I haven't seen him since January. I was especially looking forward to it because he's been on a major health kick since then too. He'd be my roommate and my only real support system when it came to what I ate that weekend. He was supposedly upstairs waiting for me so we could go to lunch. I was an hour late so I imagined he was up there chewing his cud, debating whether or not to sneak off for a quick nosh before I arrived.

The lights were off when I unlocked the door to our room. I smelled pot and heard Uri sleeping over in the corner. I saw his arm hanging off the bed with his hand cupped as if he was collecting rainwater. I quietly rolled my suitcase inside and decided to wake him up by squatting over him and gently placing my testicles in his hand. I pulled my scrotum out of my shorts and tiptoed like an insane ninja toward his bed. Just as I was about to make contact, the person in bed sat up—it wasn't Uri. It was some bearded guy named Barry who I'd never laid eyes on in my life. I was stunned. But imagine *his* surprise waking up to a fat, giggling maniac standing over his bed with his nuts hanging out of his pants. He mumbled something about being a friend of Uri's and fell right back to sleep. I made a nervous, shame-filled U-turn and headed for the elevator. A stoned stranger was in my bed, and I almost made him hold my balls in his sleep. The wedding weekend had officially begun.

I called Uri to give him some shit for not waiting in the room as planned.

"How'd you like the little Jew in your bed?"

"Scared the crap out of me. And that's *your bed*, asshole."

"Fair enough. Walk out of the hotel, make a left, walk two blocks, and make a right on Saint Charles. We're at this oyster joint called the Pearl. We're a dozen in."

"You couldn't wait?"

"What, they're gonna run out?"

"Just slow down. I'm en route."

"Move that fat ass."

"Ain't so fat anymore."

"Hey guy . . . You're *still* fat."

Touché. I was still fat. I'd been forgetting that fact lately, which in and of itself was a development. You lose almost forty pounds, you start feeling human again. That's a lot of weight to lose, until you realize where you started. I had been up to 263 pounds. He was right. I was fat. So was he.

Uri and his friend Andy were elbow deep in plates of oysters and fried soft-shell crabs. Neither mentioned how I look. I was surprised, mildly offended, and completely relieved. I ordered some oysters with a vodka and soda.

Here's a tip. If you're planning to eat oysters and drink vodka throughout the weekend, perhaps you might give yourself a base coat at that first meal? A bit of bread? Some soup? Would it kill you to eat a sandwich? Let me tell you what not to do. Don't eat eighteen oysters before you've even unpacked your suitcase. And it's no major accomplishment to have three vodka and sodas before most of the wedding guests have landed in town.

As I walked back from the restaurant, my stomach started bubbling like Old Faithful. As we approached the hotel, I was getting frantic for a bathroom with some privacy. As luck would have it, we started bumping into arriving wedding guests, some of whom I knew, some of whom I was meeting for the first time. There would be lots of folks at the wedding whom I didn't know (exhibit A: Barry). But Uri knew *everyone*. He was like the goddamn mayor of this wedding—making me the mayor's roommate. By the time we got up to our room, there were a half dozen guys with us, only one of whom I'd ever met before today.

In our room, Uri was holding court with his friends

from New York. I was dying to use our bathroom, but I was in a tiny hotel room surrounded by perfect strangers. I held out. I sat in absolute misery. I would start bleeding through my eyeballs before I'd take *this* crap in *that* bathroom in front of *those* people. No way.

One of them pulled out a flask of bourbon. It seemed we were all about to do a shot. Oh goody! Just what my body wants right now, a laxative. Anybody got a few prunes I can nibble on while I wait my turn? I fantasized about standing up and screaming at everyone to get the fuck out of the room. I did not. These were Uri's good friends. And, while I didn't really know them, I knew them. We'd be hanging out for the rest of the weekend. This was not the first impression I was looking to give these guys. So I sat there, writhing in pain, trying not to shit in my pants.

We drank.

"TO MARCO AND ANGELA!"

Yes, yes. To Marco and Angela. Lovely couple. Now please get out of here before I start crying.

The bourbon hit my throat as if shot out of a gun. Once it hit the cesspool of vodka and oysters in my stomach, all bets were off. I hadn't done a shot in maybe fifteen years. It didn't go down well. I was not physically or mentally comfortable. I was trying not to fart or sweat. Try that sometime—it's great fun. Finally, I'd had enough. I ginned up the courage to level with everyone.

"Gentlemen, this is going to be awkward for all of us," I said. "But, I've really got to use the bathroom."

"Don't they have a bathroom in the lobby?"

"You are a disgusting person."

"Do you have matches?"

"Who ordered the fat guy?"

I'd known these guys for twenty minutes. I loved them.

For the entire weekend, the only thing less important to everyone than sleeping was eating. Ironic? Yes. Annoying? Yup. I wanted to be around food. I wanted to test myself. I also knew myself well enough to know that part of me wanted to fail. I wanted to eat. Throughout the weekend, there were times when I knew that—if given the opportunity—I'd have eaten like an animal. And while it was hell on my foodie pursuits, all the partying and going out made staying on the diet far easier than I had ever imagined.

There was so much drinking, so much live music till all hours, so much wedding chaos, that I had few opportunities to make bad food decisions. There was no lost afternoon eating my way through the French Quarter. I never even entered a café that sold beignets, much less had to watch in depressed horror while my buddies tore into them like grapes.

We went to bed so late every night that, by the time we woke up, we had to be somewhere for a wedding activity. There was simply no time to be bad. It was ironic—being forced by a wedding schedule to be good in a town where being bad is so damn easy. Of course I ate at the wedding and the rehearsal dinner, but that was a tame, controlled environment. I never really failed this big food

test because there was no time to be alone. I survived . . .
by accident.

Still, I had my moments.

The worst food choice I made all weekend? I ate two
pieces of wedding cake. Normally, I don't even like wedding cake. This one, however, was particularly good. It was
moist with plenty of icing. For a guy who hasn't eaten
sugar in three months, what do you think I'd say about a
slice of cake? It could have been made out of wax and I'd
have raved about it.

As far as the war plan I made with Janet, it was a
draw—at best. We said no sugar. I blew that with the wedding cake. We said to fill up on raw oysters. After lunch
that first day, I never had another raw oyster all weekend.
Finally, we agreed that I would have no fried food. I blew
that rule to smithereens. Overall, I ate thirty or forty fried
oysters, a few dozen fried shrimp, four or five fried catfish
fillets, and a handful of crawfish beignets, which were fea-
tured at the wedding.

The best thing I ate all weekend was a fried-oyster
hors d'oeuvre at the rehearsal dinner. The dinner was held
at Broussard's, the famous restaurant in the French Quarter. I have no idea what the actual hors d'oeuvre was. Neither did the waiter—he called it "oyster business," as in,
you've got to try some of this oyster business. He was right.
It was a bite-size piece of puff pastry with a small fried oyster wedged inside, accompanied by a cream sauce littered
with crispy, cubed pancetta. It hit all the right notes. I
snatched two off his tray but never saw another waiter

come out of the kitchen with more—which was probably for the best. Believe me, I was looking. I couldn't stop talking about it all night. I'm not sure what the "business" side was, but it was sensational.

When I got back from New Orleans, it dawned on me that I had precious little time to lose the rest of the weight. Why was I so casual in the days leading up to my trip to New Orleans? Why did I allow myself to eat all that fried seafood down there—not to mention the cake? Yes, it could have been worse, but I surely didn't do myself any favors. Now that I was on the other side of the trip, all I could think about was sand falling through the hourglass before my fifty weeks were finished. Losing thirteen pounds in eight weeks? Was that even possible?

I did the math. It was a long shot. But I put on a brave face and convinced myself that it was more than feasible. I decided to keep my head down and focus on nothing but exercise and healthy eating for the foreseeable future—or until Sasha came home from school.

Sasha was excited to see me. She busted through the door and threw herself into my arms as if I'd just returned from the moon. One rarely gets that kind of reception, and I was basking in the glow of being home. This is *my* child. She is lovely because *I* am lovely. She is my spawn, my precious daddy-loving munchkin. I would do anything for her, anything at all. What on earth could this angel want? If it's possible, thy will be done.

Sasha is smarter than I am. She could feel how tight Daddy's hug was. She could sense my vulnerability, my love for her, my desire to make her happy. Daddy was on the hook. Time to reel him in.

"Daddy, I missed you sooooo much!"

"Baby Bear, I missed you too. I thought about you and RoRo every single minute. Did you know that? Did you know how much I missed you?"

"Yup."

"What'd I miss? Anything happen? How's Romy?"

"Well . . . okay. We had fun and all, but Mommy said we couldn't have ice cream until you got back."

"She said you couldn't eat ice cream . . . at all?"

"Uh-huh. Not even one time."

"Did you do something you weren't supposed to do?"

"Nope."

"Did Romy?"

"Nope."

"Then why would Mommy torture you like that?"

"Cuz we got cake and cookies at Aunt Mara's instead."

"Cake . . . AND cookies?"

"Yup."

"How many cookies?"

"Lots."

"And Mommy *still* didn't let you have ice cream?"

"Nope."

"That sounds just *horrible*. Thank God you're okay."

"It's all right. You can take us now."

"Now? For broccoli?"

"No . . ."

"For brussels sprouts?"

"No . . ."

"For tushy pinches?"

"No, for ice cream."

"But Mommy won't be happy if we go for ice cream right now—"

"Yes she will. She and RoRo are waiting in the car. Mommy sent me in to get you, silly goose."

"*Mommy* said we can go for ice cream?"

"She said you'd be so happy."

"Well, then . . . we better get going before all the ice cream melts."

"You're only kiddin', right?"

"Well, mine won't melt, because they know me already. Who knows about yours? I'll tell 'em you're with me, okay?"

"Okay, Daddy."

For the second time in a year, I walked into Wow Cow. This time, however, I was with my girls, all three of them. For the first time in years, I was just a normal guy, taking his wife and kids out for ice cream. I wasn't embarrassed. I wasn't hiding. I wasn't wearing a disguise. In fact, that day I was a peacock. I was proud of my family. I was loving all the mirrors in the place, because I could see the kids no matter where I looked.

The very same girl was there, as always. Sasha wanted chocolate and ordered it herself. She asked for a sugar cone and preemptively looked back at me and said, "I'll lick the drips before they fall." She's practically a mind reader. RoRo wanted strawberry. She's too young for a cone. The second she got her hands on her cup, she scurried to the far corner of the store in a fruitless attempt to hide her booty from any pirates—especially me. Brooke, as always, wanted a cone of mint chocolate chip. The three girls walked outside to sit on a bench and eat in the sunshine while I paid.

The ice cream girl looked at me with her eyebrows raised, waiting for my order. I felt like she was daring me to ask for the usual. Not today, my dear. Not anytime soon, either. All I wanted was a spoon. No pints. No quarts. No awkward looks. Just a spoon, please—the same one you've been offering me for the past few years. Give me *that* one. I'm finally ready to use it. I just want a bite or two of what the kids are having. That's all I really need.

Conclusion

Total Weight Lost: 46 pounds

Beginning BMI (Body Mass Index): 33.8 (Obesity "Class 1") . . . first in my class.

Ending BMI: 27.9 (Still technically overweight)

Best Achievement: Actually losing weight over the holidays.

Lowest Moment: The early summer binge while the girls were in Maine.

Biggest Surprise: I like exercising.

Biggest Disappointment: Realizing that I'm a compulsive eater.

Fringe Benefits:

- Before the project, my cholesterol was 260. Today it's 185.

- Before the project, I could do three push-ups and seven to eight sit-ups before feeling like I was going to have a heart attack. Today, I can do eighty to one hundred push-ups and one hundred sit-ups or crunches in about ten minutes. I still hate doing them.

- Before the project, I'd get winded walking upstairs from my basement office to the main floor of the house. Today, I can jog for thirty to forty-five minutes without stopping. I can use the elliptical machine at increasingly difficult settings for over an hour.

- Before the project, I was wearing size 40, and sometimes even 42, pants. Today, I wear pants with a thirty-six-inch waist—except when I don't.

- I dropped four belt notches this year.

Before the Fatty Project, I'd given up on my physical self years ago. I thought I was through. Then the sleep apnea issue surfaced and I was forced to do something about my weight. Were it not for that embarrassing CPAP mask, I don't know that I would have had the strength or interest in losing a significant amount of weight.

I haven't worn the CPAP mask in a few months now. Dr. Williams never officially said I could sleep without it. I just sort of stopped. Ironically, Brooke didn't even notice I wasn't wearing the crazy thing until a few weeks went by. How could that be? She was too happy sleeping through the night.

Almost as soon as I started losing weight, my snoring got significantly better. Once I took off the first fifteen pounds, I'd test the waters by "forgetting" to wear the mask in order to see what Brooke's reaction would be. To my great surprise, she didn't say a word about my snoring or sleep apnea for weeks. I was shocked. This was the same woman who'd taken it upon herself to tape my snoring on a regular basis and play it back to me in the morning. And some men wake up to a hot cup of coffee . . .

As I tended to be asleep when I snored, Brooke was the one who reluctantly confirmed that my snoring and sleep apnea had gotten better. She hated throwing me that bone, because it meant I might have a way out of the corner into which I'd painted myself. She had been happy knowing that I was wearing the mask. She felt strongly that the mask was vital to my health and, thus, our future. Suddenly, I was getting away with not wearing it. Removal of the CPAP mask, on the basis of the slightest bit of success, was a dangerous thing for her to endorse. If I took my eye off the ball and got complacent again, lord knows what I'd end up doing to myself. (See chapters 1 through 9.)

When I first started wearing the mask, I'd tell Brooke night and day that it was only a matter of time before I lost enough weight and didn't have to wear it anymore. She'd look at me with those big brown eyes and say something patronizing like "Sure, honey" or "I hope you're right." You didn't have to be a genius to know what she really thought. She spoke to me as if I'd told her that I built a time machine in the garage.

Once I actually lost weight and stopped snoring, Brooke struggled with the notion that my harebrained scheme might actually come together. Like it or not, I was getting better.

No snoring = no sleep apnea.

No sleep apnea = no CPAP mask.

No mask = dignity.

Dignity = well . . . dignity.

It's not that she didn't want me to succeed. It's just that she was hoping it would take more weight loss for me to get out of wearing the mask. Sorry, Charlie.

To her credit, she never lied to me. As much as it frustrated her, Brooke kept me apprised of the snoring situation nearly every day. I, however, am not as honest as she. Early on, I tried various little scams to get out of wearing it. At bedtime, I'd set it up just like I was supposed to— filling up the water tank, cleaning the hoses—making a big show of it all. As soon as I saw her start brushing her teeth or flossing, it was my cue to start the CPAP follies. Sometimes, I'd even sit in bed reading or watching TV with the mask strapped to my face—just so she'd know I was wearing it. She'd look at me with pity and say something supportive before she fell asleep. She's a doll.

With any luck, if I timed it right, I'd only have to wear the mask for a matter of minutes before she fell asleep. Once she fell asleep, I'd get rid of the mask and go about my business, i.e., sleeping like a human being. On the rare occasion when she'd get up to use the bathroom in the middle of the night and realize that I wasn't wearing the mask, I'd act confused and tell her that it must have fallen off in my sleep. I'd quickly strap the mask on for a few seconds, wait for her to fall back asleep, and then toss it back on the floor where it lived. Quite a life I'd carved out for myself.

Fortunately, at least for the time being, the CPAP mask is a thing of the past. I honestly don't know if I could have worn it for much longer. It was a hell of an incentive to lose weight, that's for sure. If all obese people had to wear one, we'd see tens of thousands of folks losing weight like never before. That mask could make anyone at least try to lose weight—even me.

Aside from losing the mask, this yearlong project has forced me to accept some cold, hard facts. Most importantly, I'm not simply a food lover who decided to write a book about losing weight. I'm also an emotional eater, a food addict, a binge eater, and a pathetically undisciplined man. *(I also enjoy long walks on the beach, romantic movies, antiquing, rainy days, jazz, and cashmere sweaters.)*

I lost forty-six pounds over fifty weeks. I didn't hit my original goal of fifty pounds, but I came close enough to call this year a success. What about those last four pounds? Well . . . they're around here somewhere.

I thought about saying that I had, in fact, lost all fifty pounds. I figured it was easier and cleaner than the truth. What's four pounds, after all? But there's very little about making this kind of lifestyle change that's clean or easy. This weight-loss thing is hard. In fact, it's the hardest thing I've ever had to do. To pretend that I lost fifty would diminish the accomplishment of losing forty-six pounds. And who's to say I won't lose the last four pounds? (Please put your hands down.)

Fifty weeks is an arbitrary period of time, set up to make the premise of the project work in a neat, marketable package. But if I learned anything this year, it's that this isn't a fifty-week gig. *My* Fatty Project is for the rest of my life. I know what happens when I'm not focused. I'm choosing not to return to that way of life. I want a different future than the one I had when I started. *That's* why I feel successful.

It's been a cathartic, invaluable year. I actually broke through some of the emotional and psychological issues that have plagued my relationship with food for much of my adult life. I'm far healthier than I was a year ago. I'm back in the game. While I'll never be totally at ease in my own skin, losing this weight has given me a considerable portion of my confidence back. I'm within the margins—where I plan to stay.

My weight today isn't anything to brag about. At six two, the U.S. Department of Health and Human Services says I should weigh well below two hundred pounds. The government also almost declared ketchup a vegetable, so take it with a grain of salt. But this project wasn't about what the government classifies as obese. This project was about finding a sane path to a weight that I could maintain in the long run. It was about saving my life.

This year, I broke a long-standing pattern of failure by setting my dietary goals at a reasonable level. I never tried to lose fifty pounds. I tried to lose a pound a week, fifty times. A pound a week was a healthy, manageable goal. I didn't try to a hit a home run. I never looked beyond that small weekly goal which was essential to my success. Had I lost this weight on a more radical diet, how long would I have stuck with it if it meant eating nothing but veggies and protein shakes? Six months? A year? I might have hit certain goals, but it wouldn't hold, not for any substantial amount of time.

I'm too lazy, too set in my ways, too interested in food to ever weigh 175 pounds. That ship sailed long ago. It's time I stopped waiting for it to come back. I love food too much. I love big red wine and stinky, washed-rind cheese and strange cured meats and pasta and barbecue and ice cream and crispy chicken ass and on and on. I want to cook. I want to eat. I want to try that new Thai joint that just opened down the street. I want to continue my love affair with all things related to pork. To permanently walk away from all those things would take away too much of myself. To what avail? Mario Batali is a hero of mine, not Jack LaLanne.

What, then, do I want? I want health and happiness—nothing more. I've certainly stopped wishing for a body I'll never have. Moving forward, I cannot be so reckless with food. But I also have to give myself permission to be who I am. I'm thirty-seven years old. This is me. I could be a lot worse. I'm kind of fun to be around. And I'm stuck with myself for the foreseeable future. Once I get to know me, I'm sure we'll become besties.

Failure—sometimes intense failure—comes when

you change your lifestyle. If it were easy, if anyone could do it, what kind of story would that be? That's not the way real life works, at least not my life. Instead of pretending away all my failures, I chose to discuss them— even celebrate them. Early on, failing was a soul-crushing, ego-bruising loop. But getting back up, and actually finding some success, started to feel good—too good to ignore. Eventually, I wanted to succeed at the Fatty Project more than I wanted to eat. It took a few times to get my act together, but I came around. I learned a valuable lesson from that.

One of the other challenges of writing this book has been willingly discussing my weight with people other than my imaginary friends—who happen to think I *always* look thin. This willingness to discuss my inner demons in public opens up a world of future book topics:

1. *Why I'm Still Afraid of the Dark*
2. *Adult Bed Wetting—We Are Not Alone*
3. *Oops! Is That an Adam's Apple?*
4. *Premature Ejaculation—A Memoir*
5. *Why Talking to Your Mom Every Day Is Cool— Even When You're 37*
6. *No, You Go See What That Noise Was. I'll Wait Here with the Cat*

I will always be the guy who wrote that book about being fat. That's forever. What's the first thing folks are going to do when they see me? What's the first thing they'll see when my wife posts her 937th family photo on her Facebook page? *(Status: Sad I have to fuck this whale standing next to me.)*

A genuine healthy-living project takes a lifetime to complete. It means slowly adjusting my relationship with food to something that is sustainable, healthy, and pleasurable all at once. This year, in all its pain and glory, was only that—a year. I grew up a bit. I lost weight. I gained back a few pounds. I exercised. I binged. I drank more coffee than Voltaire. But, in the end, it was only a slice of my life. This was a quantifiable period during which I had the luxury of thinking about my health, my diet, and my relationship with food as my job. I won a few rounds. My belly won a few rounds. In the end, I feel like I came out on top, but every few hours, my stomach demands a rematch. We're likely to be fighting this one out for the rest of our days. And that's just it. This goes on forever. If you're going to do it right—and if you're hell-bent on living a life in which enjoying all kinds of food is decidedly important to you—then you've got to be in it for the long haul. If I can live with making a commitment to smaller portions, better decisions, and basing my meal choices around a healthy variety of food, then I finally get what this is all about. Is it an epiphany? Perhaps. Whatever the name, it's a good thing. It's a very good thing.

I've used food as an antidote for whatever uncomfortable feelings I was dealing with at the time. I ate when I should have been comfortable just sitting with myself. Am I empty inside? Hardly. I'm full of life. So I have to stop using food as an umbrella against the periodic emotional rain that falls. There are worse things than getting wet.

For the better part of a year, I had a great job—taking

care of myself and writing about it. I had every reason to seek out the best advisers money could buy. Why not see a personal trainer and my very own nutritionist? Doing so made sense for my health, as well as the Fatty Project itself. In short, I had the motivation and the resources to spend a dedicated amount of time getting healthy in this decidedly white-collar way. But, what now? I don't have the budget or interest in seeing a nutritionist now that the project is done.

Thus, in the weeks after the project ended, I started attending Weight Watchers. Weight Watchers costs roughly $30 a month. A private nutritionist cost hundreds of dollars more. I don't have the nerve to say that anyone can afford the cost of seeing a private nutritionist. However, I feel just fine about saying that your health, like mine, is worth $1 a day. If you can't swing a dollar a day, God help you—but we both know you're full of it. The crap you're eating costs more.

Weight Watchers? Yup. No kidding. I'd always considered the company a bit too cultish, a bit too gung-ho, a bit too . . . pedestrian for a fancy hipster such as myself. Weight Watchers was where chubby housewives from Des Moines went after the church social, not this snobby East Coast gentleman. Well, I was wrong—again.

Weight Watchers has had quite an impact on me. It wasn't some grand epiphany. It's not a guru or a wonder drug. It isn't even David, my trainer. When did all this stuff finally click for me? The day I swallowed my pride and walked in to my first Weight Watchers meeting. How did I find myself there? My mother-in-law, Karen, made me come with her.

At the age of sixty-four, Karen is still quite a beauty. She has long, silver hair and a healthy, fit body. She's taught yoga for the last decade, so you know the type: earthy, spiritual, kind, oddly flexible, in touch with the ebb and flow of the world. You know, a lot like me.

As you can imagine, I wanted no part of it. I'm not a big fan of groups, be they fraternities, clubs, torch-wielding mobs, or fat folks looking for a shoulder to cry on. But, after a few weeks of playing possum, I relented and grudgingly agreed to attend *one* meeting with her.

There's a Weight Watchers office just up the road from my house—not two blocks from Wow Cow and McDonald's. It's one of those places I've driven by a thousand times but never noticed. I guess if you're not looking for Weight Watchers, you'll never see it. Instead of coming just a few minutes early, I got there at 11:30 AM, a full half hour before the meeting was to start.

The Weight Watchers office itself is in a little two-level, indoor strip mall. Taking a deep breath, I went to open the door. It was locked.

It was a sign from God. I wasn't supposed to be here. I was too special for this place. If I was meant to attend these meetings, why was the door locked? I know divine intervention when I see it. I turned around and started to make a run for the parking lot. Just as I was turning the corner, a voice called out from behind the glass door.

"Hey, hey . . . where you running off to? Were you looking for me?" It was a tall, thin woman with short brown hair and a friendly smile. She was wearing a red blazer and a Weight Watchers name tag that had "MAR-

GARET" written on it. "I was just opening up. You wanna come inside?"

"Not as much as you'd think."

"Come on in. I won't bite ya. First meeting?"

"Yeah."

"Even been to Weight Watchers before?"

"No. Never thought I'd see the day, frankly."

"Yeah, I get that a lot. Said it myself a time or two."

"You came here as a customer?"

"Are you kidding me? I'm a two-time loser. I lost fifty pounds at Weight Watchers, gained it all back plus twenty pounds, then came back and lost the seventy pounds once and for all. That was four years ago. All the Weight Watchers leaders are former clients. It's a rule. You can't teach here unless you successfully lost weight at Weight Watchers and kept it off."

That actually made me feel good. At least the person in charge was once a fatty too. I liked that.

"Well, I'm here to try it. I'm meeting my mother-in-law. She's been coming for a while."

"Your mother-in-law's dragging you in here? Brutal! C'mon. Let's get you signed up and weighed in before the wolves show up."

Unlike the disaster of a saleslady at the health club, Margaret was all business. She made me fill out a form and ran my credit card, all in less than three minutes. And, just like that, I was a card-carrying member of Weight Watchers. There was only one thing left to do—weigh in.

I was wearing jeans, Crocs, a T-shirt, a sweatshirt, and

a down vest. Margaret was on the other side of the counter. On my side, it was just me and the scale.

"Should I take off anything?"

"It's up to you. Do whatever you want. I've seen it all in here."

I took off my vest, sweatshirt, and shoes. I felt so cliché, stripping off my clothes so I could weigh a few ounces less for my first weigh-in. Luckily, I was there so early that no one had to watch me disrobe in a strip mall. I got on the scale. It read 219.4. Knowing where I'd come from, I wasn't too disturbed by the number. Still . . . 219.4. Big, big kid.

"The first thing you should try to do is lose 5 percent of your total weight. That's eleven pounds. Can you stick around here long enough to lose it?"

"I can."

"Will you?"

"I will."

"Then I'm gonna tell you something before everyone gets here. This works. What we do here works. Forget all the stuff we sell, the little sayings, the weekly meetings. The program itself, it works. Just remember that. It works."

I thanked her and quickly scurried into the corner. I sat down and buried my nose in the Welcome to Weight Watchers reading materials she gave me. I was trying to get myself excited about "points" and "green diamond" filling foods when I looked up and noticed that the place was suddenly full of clients.

It was 11:45 AM. Still no sign of Karen. I was hiding, and my blood was pumping with nerves. Still pretending to read, I peeked over the edge of my pamphlet to see who else was coming in and watch them as they each stepped onto the scale.

There was a long line to get weighed. I was so happy I came early, because I know I wouldn't have waited in the line. I'd have called Karen on her cell and made up an excuse. I'd rather deal with her disappointment than stand in line to get weighed. No goddamn way.

The line was 90 percent women. Most of them were over forty. At the front of the queue was a well-dressed middle-aged woman. I watched her take off her coat, then her sweater, then her turtleneck. She was suddenly wearing nothing on top but a sports bra. Next, the pants came off. Fortunately, she was wearing biking shorts underneath her slacks. This woman just stripped down to a sports bra and biking shorts in a room full of strangers. No one in line so much as blinked. She stepped onto the scale as if getting weighed in her underwear was the most normal thing she'd do today. "Oh wait!" she says, stepping off the scale. She forgot to take off her wedding ring. She pulled it off and handed it to the lady behind her. God forbid she get weighed with her ring on.

Margaret recorded the woman's weight, quietly told her the results, and the two of them high-fived. Must have been a good week—or a very heavy ring. She stepped out of line, casually got dressed as if she were in her walk-in closet, took her ring back from the lady behind her, and sat down just a few seats away from me. I had seen her in a bra. I was disoriented.

Then, just like that, it occurred to me—I was in the

right place. This joint was full of nut jobs, just like me. They too were desperate for some good news from that scale. They were just as screwed up and tortured over their weight as I was. Suddenly, I exhaled. I put down the pamphlet I was pretending to read. I sat up straight in my chair. I took off my vest. I was staying. I was supposed to be here. I was in a room full of people who were just like me. They need help. So do I. Perhaps there was strength in numbers.

I leaned forward and tapped the woman from the scale on the shoulder.

"Hi. My name's Ed. This is my first meeting."

"Hi, Ed! Is it possible that we took a cooking class together way back when? Do you know Jacques Blanc?"

I was supposed to be there.

Acknowledgments

Thank you to my friend and trainer, David Keller. You are a generous, vibrant, and unique man. I am forever in your debt.

Thank you to my editor, David Cashion.

Thank you to Kristin Powers. You personify everything that is good about publishing—and you're a hell of a dinner date.

Thank you to my publisher and fellow foodie, Judy Hottensen. You made this entire project a pleasure. Thanks for spoiling me when I come to New York.

Thank you to Farley Chase. As always, you're my trusted adviser, advocate, fellow foodie, and friend.

Thank you also to Katie Finch, Ben Feldman, Peter Steinfeld, Harvey and Bob Weinstein, Susan Berlin, Zoe Zakoutis, Erica Huss, Janet Zalman, Uri Kushner, Jessica Kushner, Toby Oppenheimer, Trevor Boerger, Stephanie

Vecchiarelli, Mara Bralove, Ari Fisher, Ben Luzzatto, Alex Luzzatto, Matthew Snyder, DeShawn Schneider-Steinfeld, and Aaron Gadiel.

Thank you to my incredible racquetball partners, Skip Holmes and Phil Ugel. Beating you brings me more pleasure than it should. Phil, thanks also for a lifetime of great material.

Thank you to Karen Bralove for your unflinching support. You give mothers-in-law a good name.

Thank you to my dad for teaching me how to fish, eat, and live. I've become good at all three.

Thank you to my mom for your love and support over this, and every other, year. You are an exceptional mother. I'm lucky to have you.

Thank you to my two bears, Sasha and Romy. I love you more than anything in the world. You are my bright lights.

Most of all, thank you to my eminently patient wife, Brooke. You are my trusted critic and my beautiful muse. I love you. You have great skin.